ACKNOWLEDGMENTS

The authors would like to thank the following]
book and to the Music Business Supplement S(
from Simpsons Solicitors, Norm Lurie and Me₁₁ₒₒₒ ....
editor Shelley Barons and our teaching colleagues, particularly Ian Miller and Trevor
McQuade.

Thanks also to Emma Driver who agreed to be interviewed for this book, and to Matt
Ellis and Amanda Easton for providing their biographical information Thanks also to
McCrindle Research and Box Hill Institute. A special thanks to our families, wives and
children and perhaps most importantly thank you our students both past and present who
are the real inspiration and indeed the guinea pigs for the ideas contained in this book.

All references to Shane Simpson *Music Business* refer to Third Edition published 2007.

MUSIC BUSINESS
EDUCATION SUPPLEMENT

MUSIC MARKETING, PR

& IMAGE MAKING

Copyright © 2006
Exclusively licensed to:
Music Sales Pty. Ltd.

Cover Design: Inblue Marketing Communications
Text Layout: Inblue Marketing Communications

ISBN 1921029420
Order Number MS04093

Exclusive Distributors:

To The Music Trade:

Macmillan Distribution Services,
56 Parkwest Drive,
Derrimut Victoria 3030
Australia

Music Sales Pty. Ltd.
120 Rothschild Avenue,
Rosebery NSW 2018
Australia

Printed by McPherson's Printing Group,
Marybourough Victoria

Wise Publications
Part of the Music Sales group of companies
London / NewYork / Paris / Sydney / Copenhagen / Berlin / Madrid / Tokyo

MUSIC BUSINESS
EDUCATION SUPPLEMENT

MUSIC MARKETING, PR

& IMAGE MAKING

Mark Beard • Ben O'Hara

This book addresses units of competency for

Music Industry (Business) Foundation

Cert III — Cert IV — Associate Diploma — Diploma

CONTENTS

FOREWORD

This series, the Music Business Educational Supplements has grown from the enormous success of my book *Music Business* – still the bible on the Australian music industry.

The Supplements do not replace *Music Business*. They have been designed by experienced teachers to assist both teachers and students to comply with the requirements of the many tertiary institutions that provide music industry courses. Some of the material in the Supplements is unique and is not dealt with in *Music Business*. (e.g. 'Marketing'.) Other material (e.g. copyright, publishing and record contracts) relies heavily on the main text.

In a sense, the difference between Music Business and the Music Business Education Supplements is similar to the distinction between doing a course and getting a job. Both are important; each helps the other; they are not alternatives but rather part of the same path - exploration and learning towards knowledge and fulfilment.

Bit too Zen for the music industry? Well, unless you are informed about the business of music it is difficult to have a long-term career in it. You can be a meteor that flashes across the sky and disappears, perhaps to be remembered fondly, or you can have a sustained career that supports your creative needs and your financial and family needs over many years. It is the difference between being a dilettante and being serious. Neither is a bad thing – but only one is a business choice. *Music Business* is a book for people who make the 'business choice'.

Because the Music Business Education Supplements are focussed on the demands of teaching curricula, they necessarily are brief and structured around units of competency. They do not attempt to be – nor do they purport to be – comprehensive. They are support vessels for the mothership - *Music Business*.

As a lawyer who has spent most of his professional life working in the business, I can say that it is always a delight to act on behalf of clients who are informed and want to know more. Their careers last longer and are more rewarding both financially and creatively. Undertaking a course on the music business shows that you recognise that knowledge is essential for longevity in the business.

Shane Simpson

Chapter One

INTRODUCTION TO MUSIC MARKETING

Learning outcomes

By the end of this chapter you should be able to:
- define marketing
- define the marketing mix
- describe the various marketing approaches taken by music managers

Defining music marketing

Achieving wealth and critical acclaim through music depends as much on the marketing as it does the music. Marketing is not something to be feared, but should be embraced by musicians, artists and mangers as a way of developing audiences and opportunities for success. Marketing, to a large degree involves communicating messages to audiences, which is essentially the role of the performer. Thus we creative people are, by default, marketers.

Creating a successful music business relies on a variety of factors. This book provides practical, street-wise music marketing ideas grounded in marketing theory used by academia and the wider business community. The university marketing graduate, for example, may not have the street smarts to deal with the often seedy underbelly of the music industry, while the self-taught 'university of lifer' often struggles to deal with the formal approaches to marketing taken by advertisers, sponsors, the media and major label marketing executives. Successful music managers are capable of wearing two hats – they are street-wise but, where necessary, can also mix in the boardroom.

It is critical for music managers to appreciate that marketing is not just advertising, selling or generating media hype. Rather, marketing is a broader social and economic process that involves matching arrays of products, service and experiences to the needs and expectations of consumers.

In today's ever-changing music industry there are great pressures on music managers. They must be good money managers, legal advisors, people managers and, significantly, they must be able to market the creative output of their artists. Successful music marketing is a deceptively simple affair. Find a great band, build a live audience and national airplay, sign a recording/publishing deal, become rock gods. Sounds easy, right? Occasionally some music managers may find themselves in this enviable position, however most soon discover that it is a long way to the top.

Artists and event marketers – strange bedfellows?

One of the greatest challenges facing music managers is the balance between creativity and artistic innovation, and commercialism. Daunted by the idea of treating the arts as a business, music managers might be suspicious of formal approaches to marketing, believing that new, innovative and inspiring events will be corrupted by the heavy hand of marketing. More critically artists often have a dim view of marketing, many believing that their creativity will be polluted by marketing.

At its core, the marketing concept is based on the principle that matching the existing needs and expectations of consumers with products and services that will most likely result in commercial success. **Creative artists** however, typically focus on the "work" or the "art" in spite of the needs of consumers. Marketers on the other hand tend to focus on the current needs and expectations of consumers. On the surface there appears to be gigantic gulf been those who create art and those who market it.

Music entertainment & arts marketing – our definition

Rather than presenting an abridged version of standard marketing definitions found in most marketing texts, the authors offer the following definition of entertainment marketing. Importantly our definition takes into consideration the unique elements of the music, entertainment and arts (MEA) marketing process.

- MEA marketing is a social, cultural and managerial process involving exchanges between consumers and MEA organisations.
- MEA consumers exchange value (money) for entertainment product (experiences, products and services) with the organisations that create them.
- MEA organisations seek to meet consumers' present and future arts and entertainment desires
- MEA organisations profit in the process.

Exchange processes in marketing

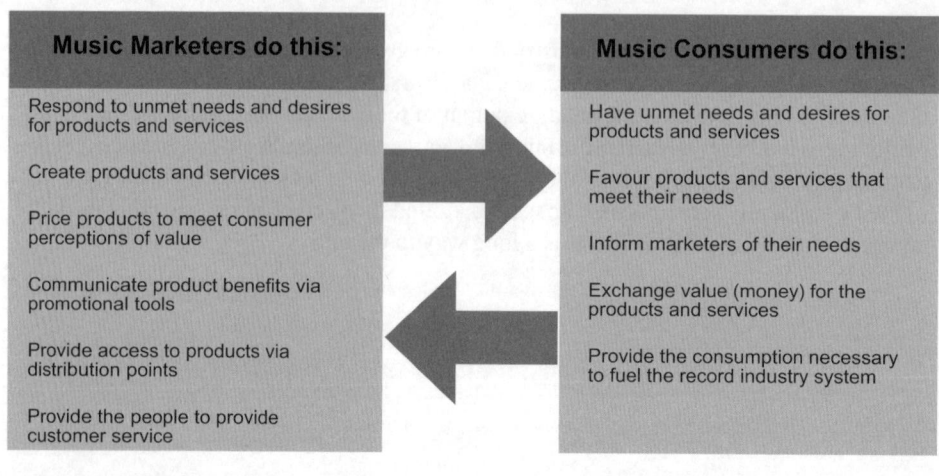

Music Marketers do this:

Respond to unmet needs and desires for products and services

Create products and services

Price products to meet consumer perceptions of value

Communicate product benefits via promotional tools

Provide access to products via distribution points

Provide the people to provide customer service

Music Consumers do this:

Have unmet needs and desires for products and services

Favour products and services that meet their needs

Inform marketers of their needs

Exchange value (money) for the products and services

Provide the consumption necessary to fuel the record industry system

The (music, entertainment & arts) marketing mix

The management if marketing involves what is commonly referred to as the *marketing mix*. This is a tactical approach that views the outcomes of marketing (sales revenue, market share) as dependent on the effective management of the marketing mix.[1] The market mix first appeared in the 1960's when McCarthy created what has commonly referred to as the 4 P's - *Product, Price, Place* (physical distribution) and *Promotion.*[2]

Over the decades other 'P's' have been added to the marketing mix in an attempt to make it more flexible to specific industry sectors. The increasing role of services in the economy for example, has urged academics to create the 7P's of services marketing, which added *People, Processes & Physical Evidence* to the mix[3]. These additional mix elements it is argued, provide for the intangibility inherent in services, but more on that later.

Critically though it is the unique nature of arts and entertainment that make the 4P's of product marketing and the 7P's of services marketing less than perfect models upon which to structure marketing plans in our industry. Thus we propose that music managers adopt the *music arts and entertainment marketing mix* as follows.

PRODUCT (VALUE PROPOSITION)		
Experiences	Products	Service

PRICE

PROMOTION

PLACE - (PHYSICAL DISTRIBUTION)

PEOPLE

PARTNERS

PROCESS

Approaches to music marketing

Customer oriented music producers

For decades, marketing theory (and practice) has been dominated by belief that the central objective of marketing is to create satisfied customers. This is based on the view that if a firm aligns its output to the needs and expectations of consumers, then commercial success is the likely result. *Customer orientation* therefore, is dependent on a firm's capacity to understand existing and potential customers.

Within the music industry the customer oriented firms are often the target of scorn. Record producers Stock, Aitken and Waterman, who produced dozens of hits during the 1980s and 1990s for artists such as Kylie Minogue, Jason Donovan and Rick Astley are a prime example. While many criticize them for their 'hit factory' approach, they created music that tapped into consumer desire for fun, lighthearted dance-pop. They clearly had a solid grasp of the needs of music consumers and didn't attempt to buck trends, rather they tapped into mood of the market and sold tens of millions of records in the process.

Artistic innovators

In the contemporary business environment there is growing evidence that marketing's bias towards the current needs of consumers is failing. To focus solely on what consumers need *today* ignores the fact that consumers do not necessarily know what they need, *tomorrow*. Collectively, consumers do not possess the vision nor imagination that is possessed by individual artists, musicians or product designers. These "creatives" try to imagine what is possible tomorrow, not what exists today. Consider Google, a firm that embraces creativity and innovation by allowing its employees one day per week just to invent new product ideas. This is not a response to consumers asking for new things they can't image, rather it is creative people inventing new ideas and experiences they believe consumers might want tomorrow. Ironically, artists might do well to adopt a marketing approach (albeit one based on innovation and creativity) to "lead" consumer tastes rather than cater to the status quo, that consumers of arts and entertainment supposedly prefer.

The job of the music marketer is to harness the innovative power of creative artists. To exploit it, yes. To bend it, yes. To manipulate it, yes – all in the context of anticipating the future needs of music, arts and entertainment consumers. In essence, to lead them to artistic wellsprings and encourage them to drink.

This is exciting news. It means that for artists to be successful they must embrace innovation and creativity. They *must* break new ground, they *must not* focus on what they think (music) consumers want today. In short, they must do what great artists have always done – ignore consumer needs and get on with the business of creating new work.

Independent musicians, such as the late jazz pianist Bill Evans, generally aspire to be artistic innovators, attempting to create music that meets their own artistic values of quality while appealing to a genre or sub-culture of fans. Early in his career Evans was troubled by the mysteries of career promotion. Not a natural self-promoter, he resolved to be the best musician he could be, trusting that audiences would find him. Evans never compromised his musical and artistic vision, and although open to new musical ideas, he always maintained the traditional jazz song structure. With this artistic approach he became one of the most successful jazz musicians of all time.

Hype-it-up approach

The hype-it-up approach is based on the assumption that the primary purpose of marketing is *demand stimulation,* in other words, the creation of markets for the productive output of a firm. Contrary to *customer orientation*, music businesses favouring the hype-up-approach can be referred to as having a *sales orientation.*

Much of the music industry was built during the post World War II period when the United States experienced massive population and economic growth. Pop culture evolved with the development of mass radio broadcasting, colour movies, television, rock'n'roll and the emergence of the cashed-up teen culture. Americans created a worldwide entertainment consumption boom. Record companies who earlier found it relatively simple to sell their products were faced with heavy competition. They began to focus more on high-pressure selling, media hype and tightly controlled distribution and retail systems to move product.

The music recording-publishing system that we know today is relatively unchanged from that of the 1950's. Only now with the upheavals created by the mp3 generation has the industry begun to pay more than a passing concern for the needs and expectations of consumers.

Ethical music marketers

Ethical or societal marketing emerged in the 1970s, as pollution, environmental degradation and recycling became middle-class concerns. No longer just the issues of the 'hippie' fringes of society, these concerns are beginning to dominate consumer attitudes. Increasingly, organisations now realise that 'going green' is not just good for the environment; it is also good for business.

If businesses can satisfy their consumers, their shareholders and the greater good of society, then they add substantially to their **triple bottom line**.

Also known as the **macro approach**, ethical marketing looks outside itself and attempts to minimise the impacts or, to borrow a phrase from the military, to minimise collateral damage. Ethical marketing incorporates environmental concerns with awareness of the social, cultural and economic impacts of business practices.

The band Midnight Oil is an example of a music business whose political/social agenda is of equal importance to the music created and the fans it is intended for. Much of the lyrical content of their songs is focused on social justice issues, and lead singer Peter Garrett is the former head of the Australian Conservation Foundation and is now a member of Federal Parliament. This is definitely a band that puts ethical practice high on its marketing priority list.

Another example is The John Butler Trio, who incorporate political, social and environmental themes into their songs, and also use recycled packaging in CD releases.

> ### Jargon Buster
>
> The bottom line of a business refers to its ability to make profits. A **triple bottom line** refers to satisfying company profit objectives, consumer needs/wants and being a responsible corporate citizen.

The chicken or the egg?

Regardless of the various orientations of music firms, one question bedevils marketers of creative product. Which comes first: the music or the marketing?

The response from artists, of course, is that without quality creative product there would be nothing to take to the market. On the other hand, the marketers would say that without a viable audience with the desire to experience the art, there would be no need to create. Most people would concede, however, that if creative artists focused solely on what people said they wanted to hear, then the resulting music would lack soul and, ironically, it probably would not sell.

After reviewing the various marketing approaches it is clear that all have some validity. All are appropriate depending on circumstances, which of course sounds like an each-way bet, but it must be remembered that marketing is a social science. This means that it is extremely difficult to "prove" anything in marketing. Success is contingent on many factors, and there are examples of both successful and successful firms using all approaches. Ultimately, though, the question of which comes first – the music or the marketing – depends on:

1. The value an artist places on his/her creative independence.
2. Whether or not the artist is releasing music through an independent or major label. Indies generally take the artist approach, while majors opt for the sales approach.
3. The value the artist places on making profits at the expense of critical acclaim, and vice versa.
4. Most importantly, the mood of the music-buying public. Music consumers are a mysterious bunch and marketers and artists ignore them at their peril!

Whether you create the music first, or identify a market niche and fill it with product, the mood of music consumers must always be one of the music manager's greatest concerns.

Marketing highlight – Approaching a music business venture

All business ventures begin with a product idea. After all, it would be rare for a music business entrepreneur to approach an unfulfilled market niche without having conceived a product or service to fill it. Typically there are two distinct approaches to developing new businesses, whether they are music-related or otherwise.

Experienced entrepreneurs

- Undertake extensive research to find legitimate gaps in the market.
- Create new products or tailor existing ones to meet the needs of the market.
- Do not enter the market unless demand for the product can be established.
- Once in the market, continually monitor changes in consumer tastes and adapt the marketing mix accordingly.

Inexperienced entrepreneurs

- Pay too much attention to product features and quality.
- Believe 'If I build a better mousetrap the world will beat a path to my door'.
- When the customers don't come, turn to aggressive advertising, sales and price discounting in order to move stock. This has the negative effect of cheapening perceived product quality and features, thereby confusing potential customers.

MARKETING CASE STUDY – iTunes playing our song

Apple Corporation, like most non-music industry businesses, has embraced the marketing approach. Unlike the perception of some in the record industry, Apple gives people what they want, when they want it, at prices they can afford – in essence they are responsive to changing consumer tastes.

The record industry stubbornly refused to accept that music consumers *want* to access music online. Fans want the flexibility of creating their own play lists, paying per song and with the ability to transport mp3 files to portable players and wireless home entertainment networks. The labels, believing their future still lay in controlling the wholesale-retail of compact discs, chose to prosecute mp3 file-sharing networks and their users rather than whole-heartedly embrace the new era of digital distribution.

The record industry is now starting to work with Apple to help sell their products, but it is important to note that it was Apple, not record companies that led the way.

An opportunity presents itself

Organisations like Apple are experts in identifying unmet needs. They identified the opportunity to create a music downloading service that would meet the demands of the new music consumer. They price music downloads at affordable, yet profitable, levels, they give consumers access to the music in formats and at locations of their choosing and they communicate product benefits (via advertising and sales) in an engaging and enjoyable way through media relevant to consumers.

Contrast this with the sales approach of record labels who try to 'hype' you into buying product that suits them, in ways that suit their outdated product formats and distribution methods. The iTunes music software and website and the clever integration with the iPod mp3 player has breathed new life into ageing record distribution models.

Study questions

1   What is the future of the compact disc as a format for music? Will it exist in five years' time?
2   Is it fair that record companies prosecute peer-to-peer file sharers who illegally download music?
3   Rock band Metallica opposes free downloading of mp3, whereas artists like Madonna and George Michael are happy to give away mp3 as a promotional tactic. What's your view?
4   Would you make mp3 samples of your music freely available on your website? Would this be a good promotional tactic for your band?

ARTIST PROFILE – Emma Driver

DIY music marketing

Emma Driver is a Sydney-based singer, songwriter and guitarist who performs mainly solo on the Sydney acoustic circuit. She started performing as a busker before joining a covers band and, later, an original duo. She has been performing solo for about five years and in 2003 released a six-track EP of her original songs called *Original Condition*.

Emma: The idea behind the EP was to recreate the 'feel' of the songs as they are performed live — without fiddling around with them too much. My producer friend and I recorded the tracks in his studio, and pretty much followed the structure of the songs as they are performed live.

Ben: What did it cost you to make the CD, and how many copies did you press?

E: It cost around $2500, including mixing, artwork and CD duplication. I pressed only 250 copies because it was a first release and I wasn't going to have it professionally distributed. I had some good advice, which was that 500 CDs is actually a lot of CDs, and when you're doing your own distribution it's difficult to sell that many. I didn't want piles of leftover CDs lying around in boxes — that would depress me!

B: How did you get the artwork for the CD made?

E: Because my day job is in book publishing, I know quite a few graphic designers. I talked to a designer who I knew had worked at a record company doing CD artwork. We talked a bit about the kind of 'look' I was interested in, then she took some photos and started putting together design concepts. It's worth having good design done, I think — people often comment on the professional look of the CD.

B: So what have you done to market your CD and how do you generate most of your sales?

E: [laughs] It's all done at gigs, and I mainly sell them to friends, and friends of friends

... basically a network of people who hear my songs and come to shows. Sometimes a stranger will buy a CD at the gig — I think the fact that it's an EP and not very expensive might help with that.

B: What techniques do you use to interest those people who don't know you already but are seeing you at a gig for the first time?

E: I always mention that I have CDs for sale, or pass around a mailing list that people can add their email address to. Sometimes I mention that I have a website, too, and that works — I've sold a few CDs to people who have been at a gig, then gone home and done an internet search to find my site.

B: How much is your CD, and why did you charge that price?

E: It's $12. I figured that six songs is about half the length of a regular album, so it's roughly half the price.

B: How did you create the website? Do you get many hits?

E: I created the website myself, because I like doing that sort of thing! I don't have a hit counter on it, so I don't know how many people access it, but it definitely picked up once it started to appear on search engines.

I've had pretty good feedback.

B: Do you promote the website directly, other than mentioning it at gigs?

E: When I send out email flyers for gigs, I always put the web address on the flyer and on the emails, too.

B: Do the flyers just go out as emails or do you send out hard copies as well?

E: Yeah, if I've got a few shows coming up, I might do a hard copy flyer and put it on the tables at a gig. It's a good reminder, I guess.

B: How many people are on your email list?

E: About 50. I know a lot of those people forward the flyers on to other people, who then show up at gigs. The net has started to spread a bit wider now.

B: How many people would you get to an average gig?

E: It depends —10 to 20 of my own crowd, plus other people in the room, on a good night. But if one stranger hangs around and listens to my set, and says they liked it, I think that's a successful gig.

B: And how many of those would have the CD already?

E: Probably most of them. All up, I've sold or sent out about 100 CDs.

B: Do you have any ambition to play in bigger and better venues, or are you happy playing where you are?

E: I'd like to play in Melbourne and Brisbane sometime. Some of the venues I play in are really great … some are not so good, and I'm starting to avoid those ones. Some pubs have music incidentally — they look like they've had their arms twisted. It's like somebody's told them, 'Put some music on here — it might make you some money', but the venue is not really set up for music. There'll be video screens on all the time, or the room won't be properly set up, or the PA will be dodgy. So I'm trying not to play at those venues in preference to ones which have an actual stage and sound system — even a sound person. These places have music because they actually think it's a good idea, rather than using it as a way of just making a bit of extra cash. Music is not my main money-making activity, so I can afford to choose the venues I play.

B: Do you have any marketing ideas or ambitions that you haven't put into practice yet?

E: Oh yeah, lots! I think I could do a lot more promotion for my CDs and for my shows. I'd also like to have my own web domain name, so that people can easily find 'emmadriver.com' or something like that. I'd like to set up a run of really good gigs and maybe take out an advert in the street press. It's just a case of how much time I've got, and how badly I want it. There's no point advertising yourself as the fourth name on the bill on a Sunday afternoon. I'd need to look at doing 'showcase' gigs and things like that.

B: What are the key factors stopping you from doing those showcase gigs?

E: Time, confidence … I'm just not sure how successful they would be. I'm not really experienced in setting up my own gigs. The way I look at it is that there are small-time musicians who are bitter about not being famous, and small-time musicians who are just not that ambitious — and I think that's me. I'm just in it to write and play songs, really. I'd rather not become bitter and complain about the lack of opportunities, or venues, or people to come and adore me at gigs. If I did more promotion and really got out there and pushed, I might have different results, but I tend not to do that because I'm not very good at self-promotion on that scale. It's all about confidence, I think.

Study questions

1 What music marketing approach does Emma take?

2 Suggest a marketing approach Emma could take to be more successful.

3 How could Emma improve her online marketing activities? Suggest three things she could try.

4 Search for Emma on the Internet. What has she done to increase her online presence?'

Marketing Plan Builder

Use the Marketing Plan Builder template to develop your music marketing plan. At the conclusion of each chapter the Builder will add a new section to assist in the planning process.

Stage one: Brainstorming your idea

Marketing ideas should be explored through brainstorming. Simply write down all your product concepts and any opportunities you believe exist for each one. Brainstorming works best when you don't judge your ideas before they have had a chance to breathe. Write down everything first and evaluate your ideas later.

marketing plan builder

www.thebiz.com.au
Download digital version of the
Marketing Plan Builder

Study questions

1   Identify a music business that customer oriented. Has it been successful? If so, why?

2   Identify a music business that practices artistic innovation. Has it been successful? If so, why?

3   Identify a music business that uses the hype-it-up approach. Has it been successful? If so, why?

4   Identify a music business that uses the ethical marketing approach. Has it been successful? If so, why?

5   If a business is to survive in today's music industry environment, what approach to marketing must it take?

6   Read Artist and Repertoire and Marketing and Promotions Department in *Chapter 17 – Anatomy of a Record Company* from **Music Business** by **Shane Simpson**. Discuss which marketing approach is used by record companies?

Chapter Two

RESEARCHING MUSIC MARKETING OPPORTUNITES

Learning outcomes

By the end of this chapter you should be able to:
- describe the role of market research in music marketing
- define the process of trend spotting in the music industry
- identify key environmental forces shaping the music market
- develop a SWOT analysis.

Introduction

In marketing, change is constant. Consumers, competitors and societies are fluid – nothing can be taken for granted. It is critical, therefore, that music entrepreneurs keep watch for emerging trends that will impact the viability of their businesses.

A major cause of marketing failure is the inability of businesspeople to deal with changing environmental conditions. A successful marketer concedes that his or her business does not live in a vacuum, but exists by the consent of the market. Successful music marketers:
- recognise change
- adapt to change
- respond to emerging threats identified by monitoring market changes
- see change not as a problem, but as an opportunity for growth
- outlive competitors who would rather ignore the consequences of change
- create a dynamic, adaptable business culture that welcomes the growth opportunities presented by change.

Defining the macroenvironment

Macroenvironment refers to the big picture elements upon which society is structured. A practical way of analysing emerging trends is to divide the macroenvironment into categories for closer study. These categories include economics, technology, socio-cultural structures and legal-government influences. Observe how these various environmental forces shape the market for music.

Environmental influences on the music industry

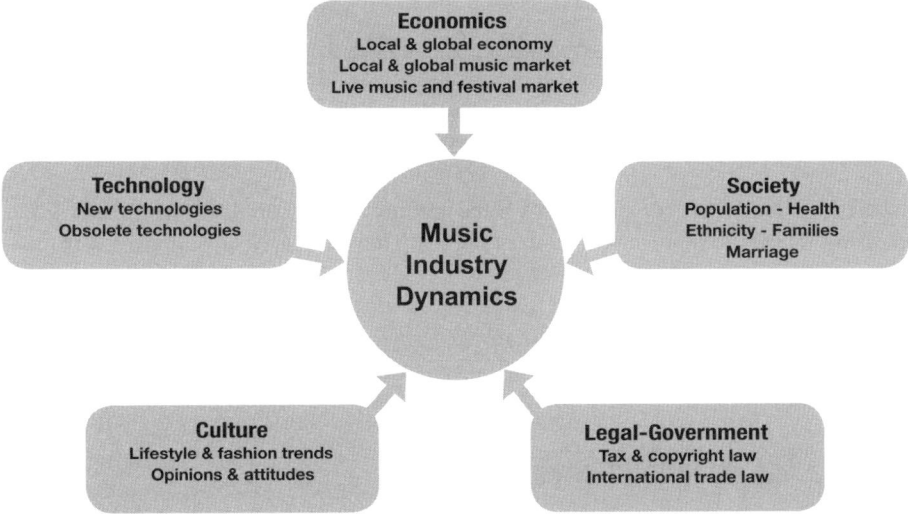

Identifying trends in the macroenvironment

Presented here are both general observations and specific data relating to trends in each macroenvironmental category. While in some cases observations have been made and conclusions have been drawn, this is by no means a comprehensive study of music industry dynamics. Rather, it serves to demonstrate the type of data needed to make real-world assessments of the music market.

Trends in the sociocultural environment

The population profile (or the mix of age groups) within a society plays a pivotal role in the purchasing intentions of consumers. Teenagers' musical tastes can vary greatly from the tastes of ageing baby boomers, for example. Thus it is critical that music marketers consider trends in population. In developing your analysis of society pay attention to:

Population growth and change – Search the Australian Bureau of Statistics (ABS) for relevant data. Available from: www.abs.gov.au.

Health and life expectancy – Australians today are healthier and living longer. The older generations have the time and the resources to indulge in entertainment and leisure-based pursuits.

Income and spending – Incomes are rising, while people's free time is shrinking. In real terms, equivalised disposable household income for all Australians, on average, increased by 12% between 1994-95 and 2000-01. (Australian Bureau of Statistics, 2004. www.abs.gov.au)

Multicultural Australia – Particularly in urban areas where the diversity of the racial mix may influence the music and entertainment purchase decisions.

Internal migration – within Australia there is evidence that significant numbers of people are migrating within to coastal and regional areas. Often referred to as "sea change" or the "tree-change" generation. Watch to see how their entertainment buying habits might be altered by their more relaxed lifestyles.

Families – Family sizes are shrinking yet the number of households in Australia is increasing. There are more single-parent families. There are more large houses with fewer people living in them.

Marriage – Divorce rates and mixed marriages are increasing. The age for first marriages is now late 20s for women and 30+ for men. The age of first-time mothers is also increasing.

Trends in the economic environment

Having an appreciation of the mechanics of economic environment is essential for all music marketers. Presented here are the major indicators to look for.

The Australian and global economy

- **Interest rates** – note interest rate movements and how they influence the ability of families with home mortgages continue purchasing entertainment products.

- **Wages and employment** – In recent years Australia has experienced low levels of unemployment. This in turn puts upward pressure on wages and in turn, inflation. People seemingly have more money to spend, yet price rises often erode the ability of consumers to spend.

- **Inflation** – in recent years Australia has experienced high levels of economic growth, low unemployment and importantly, low inflation. Economies work in cycles though. Look therefore to see possible rises in inflation as result of rising costs of living and rising wages.

- **Exchange rate fluctuations** – connected to interest rates is the value of the Australian dollar. Often when our interest rates rise, so does the value of our dollar. Consider how a rising or falling Australian dollar (relative to the US dollar for example) effects music imports and exports.

- **Business and consumer confidence** – connected to all the preceding economic indicators is the confidence of businesses to invest and consumers to spend.

- **The world economy** – since Australia operates in an increasingly globalised economy, music marketers must be sure to watch for developments in overseas markets and economies for potential impacts locally.

- **Taxation policy** – What changes to state and federal tax law will impact your business?

- **Global events** – Political/social upheavals and the policies and attitudes of foreign governments can impact upon our economic environment.

The Australian and global music market

- **Global CD sales** – Sales of recorded music (audio and music video) grew by 1.7% in units and fell 1.3% in value in the first half of 2004, compared to the same period in 2003. Audio sales fell by 2.7% in value, while the music video sector grew by 20.2% driven by DVD music video, which increased by 26.6%. Interim sales of all audio and music video formats totalled $US13.9 billion, compared to $US14.1 billion in 2003. The figures reflect a slowing of the rate of decline in music sales of the past four years. This is the best first-half year result achieved since 2000. (**www.ifpi.org**)

- **Australian recorded music market** – in the period January to June 2004, was down 8.7%, with DVD growth unable to compensate for the 10.4% value decline on albums and the 8.4% value decline on singles. In previous years, DVD growth has compensated for any weakening in the audio market. The market, however, has been buoyed somewhat by impressive results in 2004 by Australian repertoire. Following the enormous success of this month's ARIA No.1 Chart Awards, it is no surprise that local acts continue to perform strongly on the charts. Local repertoire has grown from 18% to 27% of wholesale sales value (when compared to the same 6 month period last year), which is also in excess of the 26% share reported for the full year to December 2003. (**www.aria.com.au**)

- **Independent labels** – Over 400 independent record labels registered as members of the Association of Independent Record Labels, which controls approximately 10% of the Australian recorded music market.

- **Major record labels** – Sony/BMG, Universal Music, Warner Music and EMI/Virgin who control approximately 90% of the Australian recorded music market.

- **Indirect competitors** – Competing entertainment products including movie DVDs and games consoles.

Trends in the Australian live music and festival market

- Australian music and theatre production organisations generated $620 million in income during 2002-03. Performing arts festivals generated $89m in income in 2002-03. Both ticket sales and government funding each accounted for just under one-third of the total (31% or $27m each), while fund-raising accounted for 27% or $24m. (Australian Bureau of Statistics)

- More people paid to attend popular music performances than other types of music and theatre productions (28%). Other paid attendances included: musical theatre productions (22%), drama (18%), symphony and choral (11%), dance (5%) and opera (3%). (Australian Bureau of Statistics)

- There were 176 performing arts festivals operating for greater than two consecutive days during 2002-2003, with the average duration being eight consecutive days. (Australian Bureau of Statistics)

- There has been a significant reduction in live music venues in New South Wales over the last several years, and in a significant number of venue cases, live music operations have been displaced by gaming facilities. (Johnson, B. & Homan, S., *Vanishing Acts – An inquiry into the state of live popular music opportunities in NSW*, p.1)

- According to the statewide figures on patron profiles, hotels tended to attract a higher average percentage of younger patrons between 18 and 40 years, while clubs tended to attract a higher average percentage of people over 40 years of age. In particular, an average of 31% of people attending clubs were reported to be over 55 years of age, while the corresponding figure for hotels was 11%. (Johnson, B. & Homan, S., p.23)

Trends in legal-technological environment

- Stephen Peach, CEO of the Australian Record Industry Association (ARIA), states: 'people are increasingly comfortable with accessing music in an online environment. The challenge for the music industry is that a significant amount of music is being accessed through illegitimate channels.' (**www.aria.com.au**)

- Between January and July 2003, around 3.6 million Australians illegally burnt a music CD and around 3.4 million Australians illegally downloaded music files via file sharing services. (*Understanding CD Burning and Internet File Sharing and its Impact on the Australian Music Industry* – Key Qualitative Research Findings, July 2003)

- Nielsen Soundscan reported that during the second half of 2004, 91.4 million digital tracks were sold compared to 19.2 million tracks sold during the same time period in 2003, marking a 376% rise in digital sales. (**www.themusic.com.au**)

- Legal music sites quadrupled to over 230 in 2004 with the available music catalogue doubling in 12 months to 1 million songs. Paid-for downloads up more than tenfold to over 200 million. (**www.ifpi.org**)

- Portable players, led by the hugely successful iPod, and mobile phones are helping transform the consumer experience of enjoying music and creating new revenue opportunities. There are estimates that 50% of mobile content revenues will be from music. (**www.ifpi.org**)

- Global sales of pirate music have hit another record at 1.1 billion discs annually, but thanks to stepped-up enforcement efforts the fake CD trade is spreading more slowly than in recent years. Music piracy remains a huge US$4.5 billion illegal business driven by organised crime, government apathy and corruption. (**www.ifpi.org**)

Trends and trend spotting

How the music industry uses market research

The type of market research conducted by conventional product manufacturers is not the kind undertaken by the music industry. Rather, record companies rely on trend spotting, marketing intelligence and street crew or fan club interaction to gain insights into market behaviour. See Chapter 8 for more on street crews.

For any serious research project to have valid outcomes care must be taken to ensure the ethicacy of the research methodology. This means that you cannot simply throw a questionnaire together, ask a few mates if they like your new product design and generate quality unbiased conclusions upon which to invest millions of dollars. However, this *is* kind of how the music industry works. Conversely, can you imagine product managers at Coca-Cola, Telstra or Nike making critical decisions without consulting the market? Certainly not.

In the entertainment industry opportunities appear and disappear quickly, making it difficult to use focus groups, telephone surveys and brand tracking to evaluate the likely success of a venture. These traditional methods of market research are often laborious, costly and can, if poorly designed, generate biased or inaccurate results.

Instead, record labels, for example, rely on A&R (Artist & Repertoire) Managers to do exploratory market research. This includes listening to demo tapes, checking out bands at the local pub, monitoring the charts and music press, and observing sociocultural trends that might influence people's changing tastes for entertainment.

Music Business by **Shane Simpson** - Chapter 17 Anatomy of a Record Company.

ARTIST & REPETOIRE (A&R)

Shane Simpson describes the role of A&R as follows:

Your first contact with any record company, whether a Major or an Independent, is likely to be the A&R department. This department is responsible for finding new talent and administering the recording process... The pressure to deliver hits can mute any A&R manager's sense of adventure when it comes to deciding what music to record. It is hardly surprising that until they have had a few 'hits' to their name, most simply can't take a fiercely independent A&R line.

Marketing highlight – 10 trends in music marketing

1. Indie artist topping the album and single charts – As major record labels remain focused on the forced restructuring of the industry due to the digital music revolution, they will look increasingly to independent labels to act as their 'quasi' A&R departments. Indies will find and develop the talent; majors will press and distribute. Look to fewer and fewer direct signings by majors.

2. Live music – Opportunities in live music will continue to expand as music consumers of all ages flock to more outdoor music/cultural events.

3. Faster business cycles – The life cycle of the typical artist will shorten. As in the film industry, the shelf life of a new music 'product' will be measured in months, rather than years, forcing labels constantly to seek out new artists.

4. Recording technology – Over coming years see continued rationalisation in the recording and recording studio market as the value/cost of high-end recording technology completes its invasion of the home and 'pro-sumer' market. The home studio will no longer be an exception, but the rule for aspiring musicians.

5. Approaches to recording – Artists today can be recorded and released far quicker than in the past. Inaugural *Australian Idol* winner, Guy Sebastian, exemplifies this. His first album was recorded in a matter of weeks, taking advantage of market momentum following his victory. The industry is also experiencing massive increases in DVD sales, driven by the widespread take-up of home cinema/audio entertainment. Look for increasing numbers of albums mixed in surround sound and super audio formats.

6. The retail environment – Record labels will abandon their traditional role as wholesalers. They will challenge the 'bricks and mortar' music retailers by selling direct via their own and their artists' websites. Music retailers will respond by increasing their range of DVD audio, DVD video and DVD music video, and entertainment lifestyle products such as the iPod. Increasingly they too will distribute not only CDs online but will sell digital music online, accessing product from third party digital rights managers. Eventually the CD format will become obsolete. More telecommunication carriers will enter the digital music market, treating music as mere 'bait' to sign consumers up to phone and internet contracts.

7. Media convergence – Digital consumer products will act as the centre of a consumer's entertainment lifestyle. Consider the evolution of mobile communications technology. Mobile phone, PDAs, mp3 player, digital camera, watches, video game and laptop computer will merge to become one device, posing significant challenges and opportunities for the industry.

8. The multimedia artist – will rise to meet the challenges of media convergence. No longer just singers, songwriters and recording artists, they will become stars of diverse entertainment media.

9. Compilation marketing opportunities – These will increase as classic rock and pop recordings enter the public domain when their sound copyright expires. Expect to see further manipulation of the copyright laws in the United States as the entertainment industry attempts to stop their recordings, movies etc falling into public hands, ala the *United States - Sonny Bono Copyright Extension Act 1998*. For more detail visit www.thebiz.com.au.

10. Virtual (Marketing) Communities - online communities such as MySpace will continue the new dawn they created for DIY music marketers. Coupled with online music video via such services as youtube.com, more bands will follow the Artic Monkeys and OkGo in reaching millions of consumers outside the major record label system.

The SWOT analysis

The SWOT analysis is a practical way of cataloguing issues that will impact on your business. A key function of a business plan is to help you assess whether your idea is feasible. The SWOT analysis is a widely used and practical way of critiquing the idea. It is crucial when completing a SWOT that you be honest with yourself. You cannot afford to lie to yourself or be ignorant of possible critical flaws in your idea. SWOT is an acronym for **strengths**, **weaknesses**, **opportunities** and **threats**.

Strengths

Personal and business strengths allow you to deal with the challenges presented by the outside world. They give you the ability to overcome your weakness, deal with threats such as aggressive competitors, and to capitalise on market opportunities. They are regarded as internal to the business and/or the personal qualities of the entrepreneur.

Strengths of existing business

- good management
- solid financial plan
- qualified, skilled and motivated workforce
- positive brand reputation or goodwill
- strong market share
- quality products

Strengths of new business

- youthful enthusiasm
- passion for chosen business/products
- 'can do' attitude
- ignorance of industry rules may breed less conservative entrepreneurial spirit
- previous business skills
- knowledge of the market
- education and training in the field

Weaknesses

All businesses and businesspeople have weaknesses. The wisest businesspeople recognise their weaknesses and seek to correct them. Alternatively, they delegate tasks to others more capable. Weaknesses are regarded as internal to the business and/or the personal qualities of the entrepreneur.

Weaknesses of existing business

- redundant or ageing machinery and equipment
- undercapitalisation and poor cash flow, which means insufficient funds to keep the business going
- poorly trained workforce
- workers with low morale and high turnover
- poorly trained, inexperienced management
- poorly managed financials

- management and staff too focused on products and processes, rather than the needs and desires of customers

Weaknesses of new business

- business plans too focused on products and processes, rather than the needs of customers
- lack of experience in the critical areas – financials, people management and marketing
- lack of business knowledge/skills
- lack of access to industry networks facilitating better supplier and distribution opportunities
- lack of formal market research

Opportunities

Opportunities are external. Successful businesses respond quickly not just to threats, but also to opportunities. Some examples include:
- new products for existing markets
- new products for new markets
- existing products for new markets
- developing economic, social, technological or political conditions leading to changes in consumer purchase intentions.

Threats

Like opportunities, threats are issues external to the business. The greatest threat external to a business is competition. All developed markets are filled with competitors ready to copy what you do and thus eliminate your product. You must respond to the following competitive threats:
- price discounting and price warring
- new products in the market
- entire new businesses offering similar products/services
- new promotional campaigns
- joint ventures or strategic alliance between two or more of your competitors
- developing economic, social, technological or political conditions can be a threat as much as an opportunity.

Actionable SWOT issues

A SWOT is only useful if you are able to take action on key issues raised by the analysis. You need to analyse and suggest corrective action for the weaknesses and threats raised. For example, you may have listed personal weaknesses such as lack of experience or education as hindrances to starting your own business. What will you do to turn these weaknesses into strengths? You might also list competitive threats to your business success. How will you out-fox your threatening competitors and capitalise on their weaknesses?

The following table shows that issues raised by each element of the SWOT can affect other elements. Strengths and opportunities intersect, resulting in actions that need to be taken immediately in order to capitalise. See Chapter Eight for a comprehensive SWOT case study.

SWOT strategies

Actions are required when two SWOT variables intersect.

SWOT Analysis	Strengths	Weaknesses
Opportunities	Act now. Use your strengths to capitalise on market opportunities.	Correct your weaknesses before reaching for opportunities. Tread warily.
Threats	Favour your strengths when competitors try to attack.	Act now before your weaknesses are exploited by competitors, or exposed by changing consumer stes.

CASE STUDY – Practical market research

Market research and Australian hip-hop events

What is market research?

Researching an opportunity is the crucial first step in creating a successful marketing plan. It is the link between marketing ideas and reality. It involves the collection, analysis and reporting of information that better enables marketing managers to make decisions. The basic principle of marketing is first to ask consumers what they want, then build new, or adapt existing products to match their stated desires. The key function of market research is to determine why consumers prefer one product to another.

Market research allows music managers to define problems and opportunities and assist in the development and adjustment of the marketing mix to suit a particular target audience. Market research also provides mechanisms to monitor marketing performance.

Market research has three basic functions:

1   **Description:** to describe the problem, issue or opportunity; to gather and present statements of fact regarding an issue.

2   **Diagnosis:** to find the reasons why consumers act the way they do. Often used to study the cause and effect relationship between advertising and sales for example.

3   **Prediction:** to make educated guesses – market research attempts to identify marketing opportunities.

Market research need not be complex. A music manager, for example, must regularly read local street/music newspapers and thus keep up with new bands, venues and CD releases. By using this simple exploratory research technique the manager is getting to know the local music scene and is better placed to discover new opportunities.

If you are planning an event promotion business and would like to approach a nightclub for an available night to stage a dance party, you must have intimate knowledge of the dance scene in your area. Market research is the process of becoming an expert on your scene.

Researching a live event

Music business entrepreneur and DJ, Marvin-K, is investigating the possibility of creating a monthly live music event at a local nightclub. His passion is Australian R&B and hip-hop music. Wisely, Marvin is taking the marketing approach and plans to conduct some research to assess the viability of the project before he goes ahead.

Step 1: Research purpose

The first step is to clearly define the purpose of the research. This will act like the rudder of a ship, ensuring that the data collected gives a truthful picture of the marketplace. Marvin has developed the following research purpose:

•   To determine the likely profitability and popularity of a monthly Australian hip-hop/R&B event in Sydney.

Step 2: Research objectives

Now Marvin needs to create a set of specific questions (called **objectives**) that will attempt to satisfactorily answer the research purpose. He must discover the following:

- the size and scope of the Australian R&B/hip-hop music market
- the size and scope of the R&B/hip-hop music market in the Sydney metropolitan area
- the demographic profiles of Australian R&B/hip-hop music fans
- possible venues for the event, including the venue location, capacity, production facilities, transport, access, security
- the size, scope and popularity of live music in Sydney.

Then Marvin must:
- complete profiles of all direct competitors in the Sydney R&B/hip-hop scene
- complete an analysis of the competitive environment of the broader Sydney dance music scene.

Step 3: Research design

Exploratory research
This is a technique used to gain broad perspective on a particular issue. Marvin will source information from the following areas to gain insight:
- relevant music and youth culture magazines, including Urban Hitz, Soulspin Magazine, Stealth Hip Hop Magazine, On-The-Street (OTS) and Rolling Stone
- relevant websites, including www.urbanflavours.com.au, www.araia.com.au, www.air.com.au, www.thebiz.com.au, www.ozco.gov.au, www.artslaw.com.au
- relevant academic literature, including Vanishing Acts – An inquiry into the state of live popular music opportunities in NSW
- relevant broadcast media, including Triple J, Triple M, FBI FM, Channel V, MTV and Video Hits.

Descriptive research
This method of analysis is divided into primary data collection (questionnaires and surveys) and secondary data collection (existing data that is collected for another purpose).

Primary data collection
Marvin decides the best way to gain deep insight into his business proposal is to create a questionnaire and interview dance/hip-hop/R&B industry opinion leaders.

He makes a list of club promoters, DJs, record company executives, music journalists and critics, agents and music managers. His strategy is to use an in-depth qualitative survey.

He will make appointments and try to 'pick the brains' of the opinion leaders. His questionnaire, being qualitative, will be made up of open-ended questions that will attempt to draw detailed opinions from his respondents. He is not using quantitative measures or, put simply, questions with mathematically measurable answers, for example 'On a scale of 1 to 10 rate the following...'. Rather he wants to collect broad insights from the industry professionals.

Secondary data collection
Many of Marvin's research objectives can be answered from existing published sources. Earlier, in Marvin's exploratory research, he planned to use numerous external sources to gather insight into his research.

Many of these same sources could potentially be used to gather the sales statistics, demographic and industry information necessary to answer his objectives. Additionally Marvin could access secondary data from the following sources:

Publications from government
Australian Bureau of Statistics
NSW Department of Commerce

Periodicals and journals
- Australasian Marketing Journal
- OURhotel – Journal of the Australian Hotels Association
- International Journal of Service Industry Management
- Journal of Brand Management
- Journal of Marketing
- Journal of Services Marketing

Commercial data
- McCrindle Research – www.mccrindle.com.au
- Forrester Research – www.forrester.com
- Jupiter Research – www.jupiterresearch.com
- Billboard – www.billboard.biz
- AC Nielsen Australia – www.acneilsen.com.au
- OzTam Pty Ltd – www.oztam.com.au
- Roy Morgan – www.roymorgan.com.au

Step 4: Analysis and reporting

Having collected the data Marvin would then analyse and interpret it, allowing him to decide on the feasibility of his proposed event.

Study questions

1   Should Marvin go to the trouble of designing and implementing his research study, or should he act on gut feeling and stage an event?

3   Will discussing his proposed business idea with industry opinions expose him to competition? How likely are they to assist him?

4   Should Marvin engage a market research firm to complete his study?

5   What other sources of information are available for dance music entrepreneurs?

Marketing Plan Builder

Use the Marketing Plan Builder template to develop your music marketing plan. At the conclusion of each chapter the Builder will add a new section to assist in the planning process.

Stage two: create a SWOT analysis

List the STRENGTHS of your business idea.

_____

_____

_____

_____

List the WEAKNESSES of your business idea.

_____

_____

_____

_____

List OPPORTUNITIES to develop your business idea.

_____

_____

_____

_____

List external THREATS to our business idea.

_____

_____

_____

_____

_____

thebiz – music business portal

www.thebiz.com.au
Download digital version of the SWOT analysis

marketing plan builder

Study questions

1 What is a trend and why is it important to spot one?
2 List 5 music industry publications you can read to spot trends.
3 List 5 websites that have music industry information that you can access as a means of trend spotting.
4 What is the importance of the SWOT analysis?
5 In what ways can traditional market research techniques be applied to studying music industry opportunities?
6 Who within a typical record company might participate in scanning the market for opportunities?
7 What are the major environmental forces that shape business success?
8 Why should music entrepreneurs keep abreast of changes in the macroenvironment?

Chapter Three

SEGMENTING & TARGETING MUSIC MARKETS

Learning outcomes

By the end of this chapter you should be able to:

- define the major market types
- describe the market segmentation and targeting process
- identify situations where segmentation occurs in the music industry
- develop a segmentation strategy for a music product and/or artist.

Defining markets

A market is an identifiable group of individuals or organisations that consume products and/or services. Markets can be classified as either business-to-consumer or business-to-business. While the focus of this chapter is to define consumer music markets, see page 51 for more detail on business-to-business firms in the music industry.

Consumer markets in the music industry

Mass markets

Mass marketing assumes that one product will serve the needs of all consumers. Today, however, there are very few examples of firms that practise true mass marketing. Government utilities such as power companies and the postal service are examples, yet even they are increasingly driven to target the prolific number of market segments with a variety products and services.

Market Segments

In today's business environment very few organisations offer one product (without variation) to the entire market of consumers. For reasons of efficiency marketers must offer variety according to the needs of individuals within sub-cultures. Markets need to be segmented simply because not everybody wants the same products and services. Market segments give companies the ability to accurately focus on individual needs.

The major market segments (product varieties) typically offered by Australian music retailers

Alternative	Karaoke
Charts	Pop
Children	Rock
Country	Soundtracks
Dance	Urban
Easy listening	World
Jazz & blues	

Looking at the list of major market segments above, you might suggest that there are many more genres of music than these. Of course you'd be right. Consider the dance category described in the follow table, which can (depending on who you ask) include dozens of styles which are continually evolving, merging and splitting into endless sub-genres. This multitude of sub-genres is a perfect example of the increasing proliferation of niche markets, that make it both difficult for mass marketers and advantageous for smaller more adaptable businesses.

Niche markets

Niche markets are those groups of consumers with highly specific needs that, for reasons of efficiency, cannot be served by larger firms. Niche markets, therefore, are typically served by smaller firms or micro-marketers, who have in-depth knowledge of the needs of their consumers.

Niche markets within the dance/electronica market

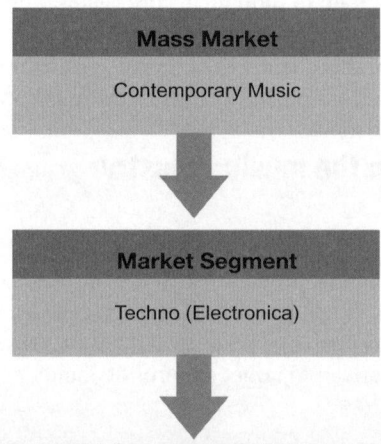

Source: http://www.ethnotechno.com/efs.php

The market segmentation process

What is segmentation?

Market segmentation is the process of dividing mass markets into groups of consumers that exhibit common or homogenous buying behaviour. Segments are then offered arrays of products and services according to their identifiable needs. Firms targeting identifiable segments can theoretically provide consumers with more precise satisfaction of their varying wants.[1] In the business-to-consumer market several variables can be used to define groups of consumers, including; **demographics, psychographics, geography, and behavioural aspects**. These provide a basis upon which to create segment profiles that can be targeted with customised value propositions (i.e. a marketing mix)

Imagine if we all wore the same clothes, bought the same food and listened to the same music – it would make for a fairly dull society. The process of market segmentation gives individuals the freedom to make purchase decisions according to their taste.

Segmentation variables

The marketing profession uses a common set of variables by which to classify consumers into identifiable segments. They are:

Geographic

Segmenting the market based on geographic boundaries such as international regions, countries, states and provinces, cities, towns and suburbs.
- *Example*: The global music and entertainment industry refers to countries as **territories**. Thus the Australian and New Zealand music markets are referred to as the **Australian/New Zealand Territory**.

Demographic

Segmenting the market based on age, sex, income, family size, family life cycle, occupation, education, religion and nationality.
- *Example*: A chill-out compilation CD might target 18–24-year-old singles with income exceeding $35,000 per annum.

Psychographic

Segmenting the market by personality type, values, attitudes, lifestyle choice, activities and social class. Watch, therefore, how we can add psychographic variables to the previous demographic profiles.
- *Example*: A dance/chill-out compilation CD might target 18–24-year-old, fun-seeking, socially active, peer-driven singles from urban centres.

Behavioural

Behavioural segmentation is the process of dividing the market into groups based on the benefits sought by the consumer, purchase occasions, usage patterns and brand loyalty.

- *Benefits sought*: Music consumers are often segmented based on specific product benefits they seek. Through its CD compilation *Cuba – The Greatest Songs Ever*, Petrol Records targets buyers using a combination of demographic, psychographic, benefits and occasions segmentation. Cuban grooves are for summer entertaining. Buyers are urged to recreate the vibe of Havana through this mix of cool Cuban grooves from the 1950s to the present day. In its review, *Vogue* magazine urges its 30-something, female, city-dwelling, **AB demographic** to serve [the CD] with lime-spiked cocktails. (Entertainment & Travel: Summer Supplement, *Vogue Magazine*, 2002)

- *Purchase occasions*: Segmenting buyers based on special occasions when they are likely to purchase. Examples include: **summertime music festivals** – East Coast Blues and Roots, Telstra Tamworth Country Music Festival and Homebake – who ensure success by making celebratory occasions on the summer event leisure calendars; **Christmas albums** – record companies encourage many artists to record and release during the festive season.

- *Usage patterns*: Consider the usage patterns of opera buffs. Many people who go to the opera have deep awareness of the product, they are brand loyal and they are heavy users. The challenge for arts organisations is to broaden their market appeal beyond the older traditionalist demographic they primarily target. Consider the following challenges faced by opera and ballet companies:
  - How do we convert non-opera goers into first-time users?
  - How do we convert occasional users into season ticket buyers?
  - How do we convert season ticket buyers into subscription members?

- *Brand loyalty*: Music fans become immersed in the sub-culture from which bands often emerge. They identify strongly not only with the music but with the fashion, lifestyle, attitudes and beliefs of the sub-culture and its artists. Unwittingly this loyalty gives the music its strongest ally – the repeat purchase (or brand loyal) customer. Like football fans, hardcore music fans continue to support their favourite artists even if they have a bad year/album.

Common demographic market segments

The following table presents six major demographic segments within western culture. They are broad generalisations that enable marketers to develop basic segmentation models when first planning the release of new products, services and experiences. They are not, however, the sole basis upon which to develop segmentation, as *all* members of a particular generation are not exactly alike. Clearly they share a common age range, however the terms given do not account for the divisions of social class, income and values, attitudes and lifestyles. For a firm to create a profile of each generation it would have to take into account the wide diversity of people that belong to that cross-section of society.

Generation	Demographic profile	Characteristics	Entertainment & media product choices
Generation Z	Born 1995-2009 Aged under 12 3.1 million people or 15% of the Australian population	Parental purchase behaviour reflects the desire of parents to educate, entertain and inspire their children. They and their children are the target audience. Older children and pre-teenagers. Impressionable consumers-in-waiting. Are able to apply pressure to parents to purchase toys and entertainment products	The Wiggles Hi-5 The Hooley Dooleys The Flowerpot Gang Sesame Street ABC Kids Mary-Kate & Ashley The Saddle Club Nintendo, X-Box, PS2 Australian Idol An emerging market for mobile phone companies and SMS services.
Generation Y	Born: 1980 - 1994 Aged: 12 - 26 4.2 million people, or 20.5% of the Australian population	The Net-Gen Teenagers	Apple iPod Mobile phones & SMS MySpace The Big Day Out Australian Idol Pop music Internet
Generation X	Born: 1965–1979 Aged: 27 – 41 4.4 million people 21.5% of the Australian population	Commonly referred to as the 20-somethings and 30-somethings. They have mortgages and are in the wealth and family building stage of their lives. These life factors impact heavily of entertainment choices. More home-based entertainment – dinner parties, BBQs.	Home theatre systems & gaming Music choices more sedate. Chill-out compilations, reissued rock/pop classic albums, DVD movies and DVD music video Beginning to focus on the entertainment choice of their young children. Radio programming – Nova, MIX FM, Triple M and increasing interest in talk & sport radio
Baby Boomers	Born: 1946–1964 Aged: 42 – 60 5.3 million people 26% of the Australian population	In the US and Australia, baby boomers dominate the socio-demographic landscape. They were the first generation to experience pop culture. These once rebellious teenagers of the 1960s and 1970s are now reaching retirement age. Many are beginning to downshift, or look for 'sea-change' opportunities to move from larger cities to coastal and regional areas.	Home theatre Buena Vista Social Club Relaxation music Rod Stewart's – Great American Songbook Real estate Sports cars Social causes
Builders	Born before 1946 Aged 61+ 3.5 million people or 17% of the Australian population.	The mature market Conservative, quiet lifestyles. A trend is emerging known as 'down-ageing', where elderly people act younger than their age. They dress young and are involved in more physical activity. Sometimes referred to as Rofies (Retired Older Rich Folk).	Dancing Older styles of music Country & western music Retirement homes RSL clubs Movement to coastal areas, residing in retirement homes where entertainment is generally indoors and sedentary. Spend their money on retirement, leisure pursuits and entertainment, travel, clothing. They also spend money on their own grown children and grandchildren.

Source: ABS Population Pyramid 2006 & McCrindle Research Study 2006

Multi-attribute segmentation

Rarely do marketers use only one or two segmentation variables to define a target audience. Rather, several consumer attributes are combined to develop detailed segment profiles. These multi-attribute profiles combine many of the previously mentioned bases for segmentation to create in-depth profiles of entertainment audiences. Consider the approach of Opera Australia to multi-attribute segmentation.

Opera Australia

Opera Australia is the vibrant identity for Australia's national opera company. Opera Australia was created through the merger of The Australian Opera and Victoria State Opera, in 1996, to create the busiest opera company in the world – a company which bears proud traditions of artistic excellence and popular appeal. (**www.opera-australia.org.au**)

Opera Australia tends to approach segmentation from three perspectives:

1. Demographic – psychographic
- Over 55 years, well-educated empty-nester couples who are visible achieving professionals (AB demographic) with combined incomes exceeding $100,000 per annum.

2. Behavioural – occasions
- Current subscribers and season ticket buyers.

3. Behavioural – usage rates and benefits sought
- Occasional opera goers interested in mainstream works such La Bohéme and Madame Butterfly.
- Opera enthusiasts interested in lesser-known operas which Opera Australia stages for reasons of artistic integrity. (**www.auspost.com.au**)

MINI CASE STUDY – The Upwardly Mobile AB Demographic

The 'AB demographic' is a term used by the media-advertising industry to classify a demographic categorised as high performing, well-educated, managerial, executive or professional people. They are well-paid yet time-poor. They enjoy wealthy lifestyles and are keen consumers of luxury, leisure, travel and technology products. Their diet of television viewing includes sport, comedy, movies, leisure programs, special events and news and current affairs programs, all of which they use as an antidote to their stressful, if well-paid, lifestyles.

Study questions

1   How old are ABs? Are they Baby Boomers, or would there be Generation Xers in the AB demographic?
2   What music would the ABs generally prefer?
3   What live music events would ABs most likely attend?
3   Do you think they would own mp3 players?
4   Are they likely to purchase mp3 on the web, or buy CDs from a store?
5   Would they buy music DVDs? If so which artists/genres might they prefer?

Targeting identified market segments

Once the market has been segmented you must decide which segments you will target. How many of the segments are suitable to your current product range and business strengths?

Targeting a single segment

For most bands the choice of which market to target should be fairly obvious. A metal band, for example, will most likely target metal fans. Rappers will usually choose to satisfy the music demands of urban street cultures.

Concentrating on a single market segment can be problematic. Consumers are mysterious and fickle. They change tastes quickly and often without reason, making the single segment strategy a risky one. Take for example the music genre (or market segment) commonly known as **rap-metal**. Exponents of this style include Linkin Park and Limp Bizkit, who, during the 1990s, blended metal and rap with huge chart success. Like any fad, however, the music soon became 'uncool' to all but core fans. Once teenagers saw it as uncool, the style and many of the bands were abandoned by major record labels.

Market specialisation

Market specialisation requires that a firm selects a variety of market segments and offers different products and marketing mixes for each.

Single product, many segments

This is the approach of firms that specialise in creating one product that is marketed to several market segments. Any artist with broad cross-over appeal falls into this category.

Cross-over appeal

Recording artists Casey Chambers and Shania Twain have not only captured the imagination of their core fan base of country music devotees, but have crossed over into the mainstream charts. Moreover, they are regarded as pop acts.   .

In the twilight of his career, Rod Stewart has reinvigorated his market appeal by releasing albums of jazz standards. His market of ageing baby boomers, who once rocked out to his earlier hits, now prefer the cooler moments of his *Great American Songbook* release. The segments he targets would now include:

- conservative baby boomers and seniors who are only interested in jazz classics
- existing baby boomer fans who are newly interested in jazz
- generation X fans who grew up with his rock/pop hits of the 1970s and 1980s.

Many products, single segment

Record labels often market similar artists within the same market segment (or genre of music). Warner Music Australasia, for example, has several artists targeting the same audience of older female teens and female adults, with introspective female singers/ songwriters such as Michelle Branch, Jewel and Natalie Merchant.

Blanket coverage – many products, all market segments

This is the approach taken by both major and large non-major record companies who attempt to offer products in all segments of the music market.

Recently, major record labels Sony and BMG merged to form a single company that now controls around one quarter of global music sales and, like all major record labels, Sony/ BMG uses the **market specialisation strategy**.

This means they either create and/or develop artists and the sub-labels through which to market them. Alternately they acquire single-segment independent labels and their artist rosters. These smaller labels have catalogues that the majors see as attractive money makers, and they either absorb the smaller labels into their product line or become distribution partners of the smaller label.

Sony/BMG's sub-labels include:

Arista Records
BMG Classics
BMG Heritage
BMG International Companies
Columbia Records
Epic Records
J Records
Jive Records
LaFace Records
Legacy Recordings

Provident Music Group
RCA Records
RCA Victor Group
RLG - Nashville
Sony Classical
Sony Music International
Sony Music Nashville
Sony Wonder
Sony Urban Music
So So Def Records
Verity Records

Music Business by **Shane Simpson** - Chapter 17: Anatomy of a record company. Simpson describes the functions of the various departments within the label structure.

CASE STUDY – Contemporary radio market segments

Critical to successful segmentation is the creation of differences between you and your competitors. The FM radio market is a good example of how broadcasters attempt to differentiate themselves by targeting specific segments of the listening public. Although the following examples are from various geographic markets, they serve to demonstrate the segmentation concepts used by radio broadcasters.

Triple j is all about the music. That's all we're here for. New music from Australia (c'mon Aussie) and around the world. The best. The most cutting edge. The now-est sounds you'll hear anywhere. If it's new and it's cool, we can't wait to play it. Bring it on! We play it first, sometimes months before commercial radio. While they play it safe, we just play it. We don't tend to have many oldies listening. Triple j is here to represent young people's musical and cultural requirements, and no-one else's. (http://abc.net.au/triplej/about/about.htm)

Triple M has entrenched itself as the station in Sydney for 25-39s. While dominating most under 40s demographics, Triple M has achieved huge results recently across Morning, Afternoon and Drive time, and has benchmarked its Breakfast shows as the best in the country. (www.austereo.com.au/profiles)

2Day FM has a contemporary format, playing current hits, ballads, pop, dance and all of today's best music. 2Day FM is a 'listener driven' radio station, primarily targeting the 18-44 demographic (female skew). Programming and station promotions are focused and developed based on the needs and aspirations of our listeners. (www.austereo.com.au/profiles)

FOX FM playing current chart songs, music from the 90s and high school hits, offers a 'hot' adult contemporary format, current hits and dance with guaranteed variety. FOX FM is a 'listener driven' radio station, primarily targeting the 18-39 demographic (female skew). (www.austereo.com.au/profiles)

MIX 94.5 is the only radio station in Perth exclusively targeting the 25-54 or baby boomer audience. Extensive research has shown that the baby boomers of today are vastly different from their parents at the same age. The baby boomers grew up in the most exciting period of the last century. The 1960s and 1970s were times of change and music played a big part in this mini revolution. The research clearly shows that today's baby boomers have money to spend and they are willing to spend it. They want to wear good clothes, drive nice cars, own big homes and dine in fine restaurants. They follow trends and refuse to slow down. (www.austereo.com.au/profiles)

NOVA 96.9 targets the under 40-year-old market with a broader cross-section of music than the narrow defined market, say, of Triple j. Dan Bessant, the music director at radio station Nova 96.9, says most listeners to the station aren't interested in music genres per se. If they love a song, it doesn't really matter if it's gangsta rap, nu jazz or western swing. (Jinman, R., 'Inside the label babble', Sydney Morning Herald, 7 February 2004, p.31)

Study questions

1   Evaluate the segmentation strategy of each of the radio stations.
2   The station profiles seem to have a consumer-centric approach. In your opinion, how well do these stations follow this 'listener driven' approach?
3   What's your opinion of the Nova approach? Do listening audiences want variety regardless of niche genres of music?

marketing plan builder

Marketing Plan Builder

Use the Marketing Plan Builder template to develop your music marketing plan. At the conclusion of each chapter the Builder will add a new section to assist in the planning process.

Stage three: Writing a target audience profile

Critical to a successful marketing plan is the development of a concise, accurate target audience profile. One simple way to approach a profile is to answer a number of simple questions.

Who is your market? (describe their age, sex, income, education, level and family situation)

_____

_____

_____

Where do they live? (geographic info)

_____

_____

_____

What are they like? (psychographics – personality, lifestyle, attitudes and values)

_____

_____

_____

_____

What benefits will customers seek from you? (behavioural elements)

_____

_____

_____

_____

_____

_____

○○○　thebiz – music business portal

www.thebiz.com.au
Download digital version of the
Marketing Plan Builder

Study questions

1   Identify the four major bases or segmentations.

2   Identify the three major types of markets on which firms can focus.

3   Identify a music business that uses the **mass market approach** to segmentation. Has it been successful? If not, why?

4   Identify a music business that uses the **product variety approach** to segmentation. Has it been successful? If not, why?

5   Identify a music business that uses the **niche marketing approach** to segmentation. Has it been successful? If not, why?

6   Should artists with strong audience support in a specific genre of music strive for cross-over appeal in other segments? Cite an example and give reasons for and against.

7   Why can targeting a single segment (or genre) of the listening public be problematic?

Chapter Four

DEVELOPING MUSIC PRODUCTS, SERVICES, BRANDS & MARKET POSITIONING

Learning outcomes

By the end of this chapter you should be able to:
- describe music products, service offerings and experiences
- describe value propositions
- define the product/service life cycle.
- define the role of market positioning for music products
- identify the role of brands in music marketing.

The scope of music products, services and experiences

Remember that in Chapter one; we proposed that music entertainment and arts marketing be defined differently than conventional marketing definitions. One of the principle reasons for this is the way conventional marketing definitions categorise a firm's offerings as either products *or* services. Yet music, entertainment and the arts are often products, services, people and experiences – sometimes all rolled into one.

In conventional product marketing, for example, a can of soft drink is relatively simple to manage compared to a living, breathing artist. Unlike artists, soft drink does not have artistic sensibilities. It doesn't mind if you change its packaging. It doesn't care if you attach it to other products, services or social causes it doesn't agree with. Unlike humans, you are free to market soft drink without emotional complications. Services marketing on the other hand, deals entirely with intangible experiences. Hairdressers, lawyers and airlines, unlike product manufacturers sell mostly the experience.

Am I product, a service, or what?

Whether the music business you are engaged manufactures products, produces service or some kind of hybrid depends entirely upon context. You might be an artist seeking clarity on how to market your music. You might be a budding record label owner who views artists and their CD's as products. Or you may be a recording engineer marketing your *services* in a business-to-business context both to artists and record labels.

Therefore rather than present one product-service model that attempts to classify all types of music businesses as either products or services, we will present models which show the *value propositions* offered by sectors with the music business.

Music business value propositions

A *value proposition* is a relative recent term that is used to describe the totality of all products, services, experiences and customer service offered by a firm to a market segment. The *proposition* part is that which is exchanged with the consumer, while the *value* part is the importance or usefulness of the proposition to the consumer. Firms increasingly use the term value proposition since they realise that the line traditionally used to delineate between products and services is blurring.

The models of music industry value propositions presented later in this chapter include various combinations of the following elements.

Products

Products are tangible, meaning they can be physically owned and have utility value. To buy a car for example is to own a product, whereas to hire the same car would be the purchase of a service.

Recently due to increasing "sameness" between competing products, marketers have looked to branding as a way to differentiate through intangibility rather than utility. They attempt to give their inanimate products human-like characteristics such as personality, purpose, philosophy and vision. The personification of products via branding began in the early 1960's when Theodore Levitt coined the term, "marketing myopia' to describe firms that concentrated too much on product, rather than customers' intangible, emotional needs. Levitt used the example of the US railway industry whom he described as being railway oriented, not transportation oriented; "they were product oriented instead of customer oriented".[1]

Conventional descriptions typically therefore, include three components to account for the apparent "depth" a product has. They are: **core benefits**, **physical product features** and **augmented product**.

Core product values:	Are the intangible qualities or core emotional reasons why the customer wants the product. Core reasons why people buy music include enjoyment, excitement, escapism, enlightenment, messages, a sense of belonging (to a subculture) and rebellion against authority – or as Dewey Finn (Jack Black's character in the movie *School of Rock*) states – 'stickin' it to the man'!
Physical product:	Is the mixture of tangible components on offer, including **shapes**, **sizes**, **packaging**, **colours**, **brands** and any other tangible element of the product. In music marketing physical products are the formats that carry the music. Examples include compact disc, CD single, mp3 and DVD. Too often though, music managers (and indeed their record labels) pay more attention to physical product attributes.

Augmented Product   Means to enhance a product's attractiveness to buyers. This is typically achieved through customer service, warranties and guarantees, after sales service, exclusive offers, frequent flyer points and VIP and street-crew memberships. The three main objectives of augmented product offerings are:

- to encourage customer loyalty and therefore repeat purchase
- to differentiate the product offering from competition
- to make the tangible products more intangible;
- to raise the emotional connection the buyer has to the physical product.

Services

A **service** is any act or performance that one party can offer another that generally does not involve the transfer of a physical good or item.

Services differ from products due to several unique characteristics, including their; *intangibility, inseparability of production and consumption, homogeneity of quality* and *perishability.*[2]

Intangibility refers to the fact that services cannot be touched, tasted, smelled, seen or heard before they are purchased. A music business lawyer for example when offering advice on contract negotiations is performing an intangible service. Equally a recording studio offers an intangible service, not a physical product.

Services can generally be divided into groups, or **sectors**:
- **Government services**: including such areas as education, health, police and military services.
- **Non-government non-profit**: often referred to as non-government organisations (NGOs). These include churches, charities and aid organisations.
- **Private sector services**: airlines, banks, insurance companies, private health services, private education, business-to-business services such as accounting and law and art, entertainment, tourism and leisure industries.

Inseparability of production and consumption refers to the fact that services are produced and consumed simultaneously. This points to critical role *people* and *processes* in the successful delivery of services. It is also the reason why these two elements are often added to the marketing mix (4 P's) especially by service firms. See page 135 for more detail.

Homogeneity of quality is a fancy way of saying that services are all the same. What distinguishes one airline from another, one hairdresser from another? They may not all be the same, but the key point is that services, unlike products are not industrial property. This means they cannot be trademarked. Product manufacturers can own a design, patent or trademark that gives you advantage over their competitors, whereas services providers cannot. Take an airline that puts a game console in the back of every seat in order to attract more customers. Seeing the idea, other airlines follow suit. This then erodes any competitive advantage the first airline had. This "sameness" in offering is what homogeneity of quality means.

Music Business by Shane Simpson - Chapter 1 - Selecting and Protecting a Name Simpson describes the purpose and process of trademark registration.

Perishability refers to the fact that unlike physical products such as compact discs, unsold services cannot be placed back in the cabinet and sold tomorrow. Concert tickets for example, that remain unsold, cannot be stored once the concert is over. The physical printed ticket obviously can be, but the empty seat is and its potential revenue is unrecoverable inventory.

Strategies used by entertainment companies to get around the problem of perishability include:

- **Half price ticket vendors** sell concert tickets on the day of the show for half the box office price. This enables the concert promoter to get at least some money for what would otherwise be empty seats and unrecoverable revenue.
- Cinemas often use **differential pricing**, or lower prices, on slow days to encourage demand.

Experiences

Entertainment, whether it is consumed in the form of a CD, a concert, an exhibition or a video game is intrinsically experiential – or experience based. A concert for example, could easily be classified as a service since it fulfils the criteria of one, (i.e. intangible, perishability, inseparability, etc) yet a concert shares little in common with a haircut, a legal consultation, dental work – all considered to be services. While the customer service experience plays role in ensuring that your trip to the dentist is tolerable, you don't go there to enjoy yourself.

Entertainment on the other hand, is all about experiencing enjoyment and enlightenment, and for this reason we see *experiences* as the core element any *value proposition* designed for the music, entertainment and arts market.

Service – (customer service)

Service, or customer service is distinguished from services in that, whether the firm sells products, services or experiences all must consider how they will directly service the needs of customers.

Like a dentist, music marketers also rely on people to deliver customer satisfaction. The human element is the core of customer service. The people and the processes by which they deliver customer service is a key element in the development and maintenance of customer relationships.

One of the challenges of running a concert tour for example, is ensuring that every show is a memorable one. The band must deliver the best performance it can every night so that all fans receive the same high level of customer service. The reality, however, is that customers (concert goers) will receive varied experiences at different concerts because events such as these are complex exercises involving many people with varied commitment and abilities in dealing with a customer-driven experience.

Music industry value propositions

The artist as entertainment product

As stated earlier, the core of a band's offering is the experience they provide either to the concert-goer or to the purchaser of a recording. The tangible product (compact discs, mp3 etc.) is simply the medium by which the experience is translated to the customer. This concept is at the heart of the current turmoil regarding the management of digital music, since record companies are wholesalers of physical product (CDs) whereas consumers just want to experience the music, regardless of how they "physically" obtain it.

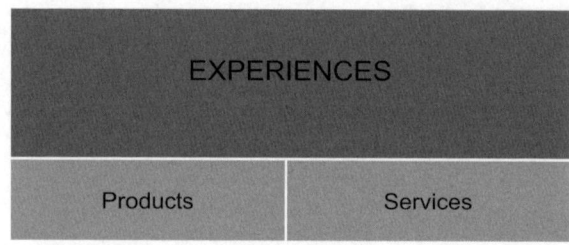

Artists cannot however simply rely on live performance revenue as their sole means of income. They must record their music and sell compact discs or digital files. They must also merchandise their brand by licensing (to lend for a fee) their name, image and music to as many product manufacturers as possible. As groups such as The Wiggles have proven, merchandising provides significant additional revenue for a band.

Perhaps less obvious is the role that customer service plays in the life of a band. Yet, if we view a fan-base as a group of consumers with whom the band should maintain a relationship with then the link is clear. A band is a business, with customers who have needs and expectations. This is not to say (as discussed in Chapter One) that the creative artist must produce whatever customers want, only that via the Internet, customer relationship management (CRM) technology, street-crews and post-show "meet-and-greets" artists must look to form direct relationships with their fans. (See Chapter 8 for more on direct marketing and CRM)

Music Business by **Shane Simpson** - Chapter 27: Merchandising
Simpson discusses the legalities of securing profitable band merchandise agreements.

A record label value proposition

The central role of a record label is to record and manufacture music and then to wholesale it to music retailers. The heart of their value proposition is therefore, physical product. The service component is realised in how they service their retail customers.

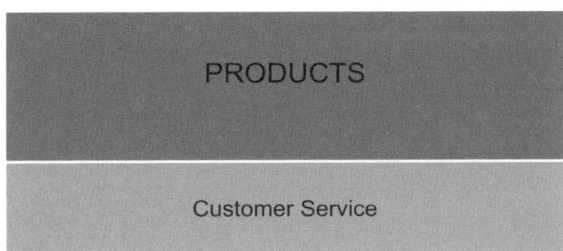

Business-to-business service firms

A large proportion of the commercial activity within the music industry occurs within business-to-business (B2B) relationships, and the predominant activity of many of these firms is the production of services.

Examples include; recording studios and record producers, music managers and agents, music business lawyers, music publishers, event managers, venues, music press and music broadcasters, video and film production companies, web and graphic design firms and royalty collection societies to name a few.

While it is true that many service firms do produce some physical products in the process of producing services for other businesses, tangibles are not their main game. Also like customer-oriented businesses, service firms must pay particular attention to how they treat their customers. Relationship management is critical in the B2B market.

Product life cycles

Not unlike living organisms, products apparently have a life cycle. Like organisms, products are conceived, they are born, they grow, mature and prosper and at some point they die.

This biological metaphor led marketing academics in the 1960's to develop the *theory of product life cycle*.[3] This model is most often expressed in graphical form with *time* on the *x-axis* and *sales* on the *y-axis*.

The classic product life cycle

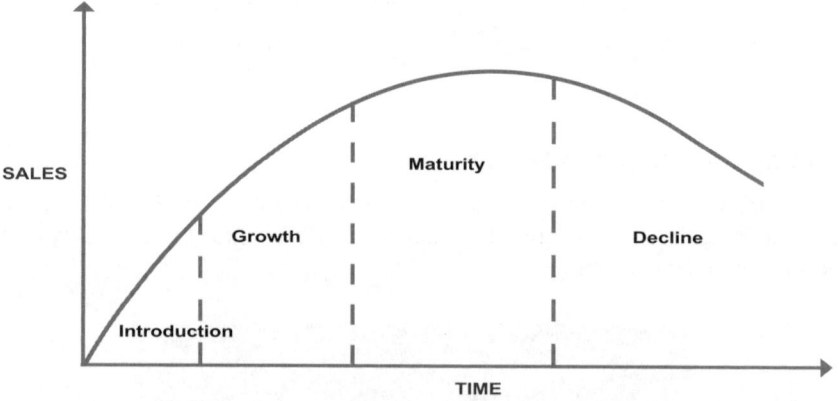

According to the product life cycle (PLC) theory, there are four distinct "life" stages through which products pass. They are:

Introduction:	When a product is released its viability is questionable. To gain a foothold the product must overcome **low growth** and **low market share**.
Growth:	As demand for the product grows, it shoots like a star. **Sales rise dramatically** as does its relatively small market share. Competitors and copycats are taking notice and begin combative actions.
Maturity:	In the mature stage, **sales growth declines** and **percentage of market share stabilises**. Such products are often referred to as **cash cows since** they can be "milked" of cash through gentle nurturing, rather than aggressive promotion. Mature markets are those where new entrants are few and the market is divided amongst **strongly established competitors**.
Decline:	**Sales and market share diminish simultaneously**. The dwindling performance of products in the decline stage has led many to describe them as **dogs**. Firms often arrest the decline by re-positioning the product (more on this later).

How to apply PLC theory?

Although this is a widely used model, its strength lies in viewing marketing activity in retrospect. This means that rather being a predictive tool, it is most useful in observing the past performance products and relative impact of environmental conditions and management decisions on the life of the product.

Consider the following graph depicting the observed life cycle of the US recording industry and its decline coinciding with the growth of internet downloading around 1999-2000.

Product life cycle of the US sound recording industry, demonstrating sales of record music from 1989-2003

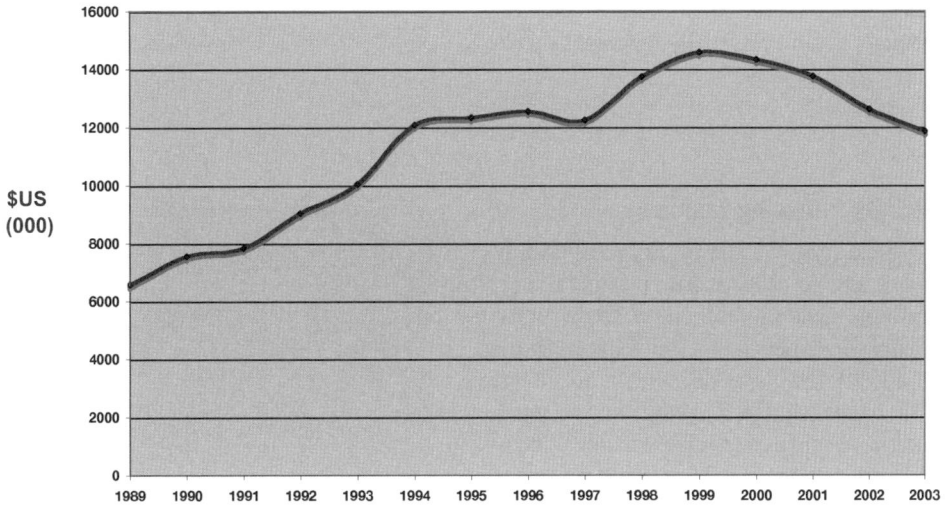

Source: The Record Industry Association of America

Observed music product life cycles

Artists reinventing themselves

It is often said that artists like Madonna, David Bowie, U2 and Kylie Minogue have the ability to reinvent themselves. Periodically they have 're-positioned' themselves, halting the decline of their product life cycle.

This re-invention is the management of **style**. An artist with style is one with a deeper sense of cool – they appreciate the need not to follow market trends, but to lead the market with their artistic vision. All dogs have their day though, and are eventually replaced by a new generation of artists.

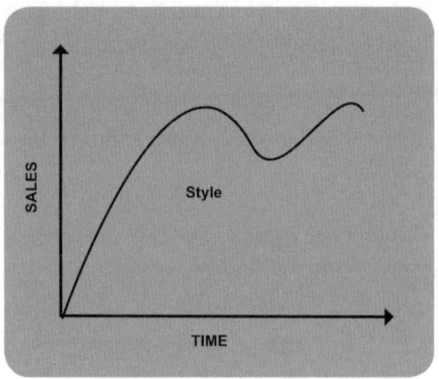

Artists following fashion

While a style can last for decades, fashions come and go. With shorter product life cycles, fashions generally fall out of favour when too many consumers adopt the fashion. During the 1990s the major fashions in music were boy bands, rap/R&B, grunge and country music. While it is still fashionable to be a country or a rap/R&B artist, grunge and boy bands have been replaced by good old-fashioned rock.

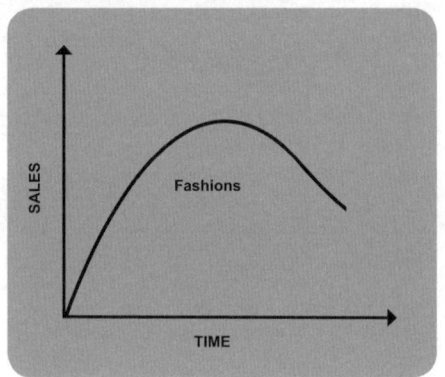

One hit wonders (fads)

Fads are adopted by audiences with great enthusiasm and then are quickly abandoned for the 'next big thing'. With short product life cycles, the faddish one-hit-wonder band may seem like an attractive money earner. This however, this is not strictly true. While it is true that any hit song, regardless of its origin, can generate huge profits, record labels prefer artists that can achieve multi-album success. An artist with a 10-album career is likely to be more profitable than 10 individual one-hit wonder albums.

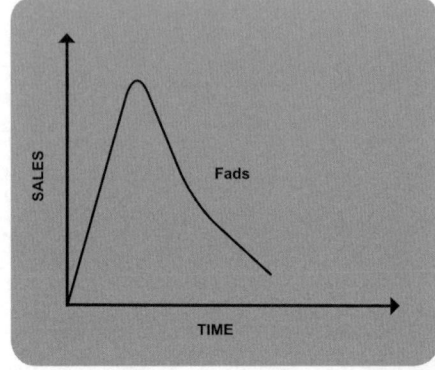

Marketing highlight – Product life cycle and single releases

Record companies know from experience that once released, a single has a limited life. Yet questions remain. How long is the product-life-cycle of the typical single? Can the stages defined by PLC theory be identified in the life of a single release? What effect will various marketing "inputs" have on the life of the single?

Partly to answer these questions marketing academics Meenaghan and Turnbull examined 22 new single launches in the UK market. Ten were regarded as successes and ten were regraded as failures. In this study they measured the effect that marketing activities such as radio and TV airplay, radio and TV airplay advertising, sampler CDs and publicity had on the sales, radio airplay and chart position of each single.

Their key findings were:

- Singles typically had a 16 week product life cycle that exhibited "faddish" behaviour.
- The shape of a music single's PLC complied with the typical curve shown on page 52.
- Over the cycle, paid-for advertising appeared to have little effect on sales whereas chart position and publicity are the main drivers of sales.
- A single is a "fashion" product whose life cycle is extremely short, yet its sales curve that follows the shape of the classic life cycle curve, albeit with a limited maturity stage.
- PLC suggests that managers can influence the shape of the curve, yet many of the factors affecting a new record release are beyond the control of the manager.
- PLC theory suggests that profits are highest at the growth stages, yet in the record business the profits are greatest in the peak (maturity stage) where the company is spending little or no money on promotion.

Source: Meenaghan, A. & Turnbull, P.W. (2001) 'The Application of Product Life Cycle Theory to Popular Record Marketing'

Market positioning

Positioning defined

Positioning refers to the process whereby consumers visualises *brand X* in relation to *brand Y.* It is has two dimensions:

1. How consumers compare brands.
2. How firms manipulate their marketing mix(s) in order to differentiate themselves from competitors and thus occupy a distinctive place in the minds' of consumers.

Not to be confused with a physical location like a street address, market positioning as Day and Wensley describe, *"focuses attention on the nature of territory over which the competitive process evolves and the impact and effect of different positioning strategies of individual firms".*[4]

How are outdoor events such as Homebake positioned?

An event organiser seeks to present compelling reasons why consumers should attend their event over a similar competing one. They do this by differentiating (making different) their offering. That way, consumers can compare the offerings of the various festivals and 'position' them differently in their minds. In the case of Homebake, it is positioned as an outdoor summer showcase of exclusively Australian music.

Developing positioning strategy

Product differentiation

Product differentiation is the "nuts-and-bolts" of finding a unique market position. It is the process of altering, adjusting or adding (or subtracting) value to your product to demonstrate difference from competing products.

Differentiation is more than just adding 'bells and whistles' to your product, rather it is the process of developing true uniqueness. A **unique selling proposition** (USP) is a unique feature that establishes your market position. Strong positioning statements require that you establish differences between your products and those of your competitors.

Is your USP really unique?

Here are ten questions you should ask of your market positioning strategy.

1. Is it relevant?	The differences you create must be valued by a sufficient number of customers. Being different for the sake of it isn't enough.
2. Is it different?	Offerings must be genuinely different. What compelling reason is there for customers to switch from their existing brand to yours?
3. Will they care?	Your point of difference must be truthful. Claims must not be empty, otherwise consumers will see through your "spin".
4. Get emotional?	Consumers must make a lasting emotional connection with your brand.
5. Are you the best?	Superior quality alone is not enough to ensure market dominance. Quality is relative to consumer expectations.
6. Can you say it?	Every aspect of promotion should contain your differentiating idea presented in an easily digestible form.
7. Who are you?	Define your brand's values, identity and personality.
8. Are you innovative?	Competitors will think nothing of stealing your ideas and calling them their own. Pre-emptive positioning based on innovation cannot be easily copied.
9. Can *they* afford it?	Can buyers afford to pay for the difference? Improvements to products can be costly, resulting in higher prices.
10. Can *you* make a profit?	The reverse of affordable – there must be sufficient profit margin once you have created your differences.

Positioning statement examples

A positioning statement is a short sentence, slogan or word that defines the market position of a brand, product or service. Ideally, positioning statements reflect a product's differentiation strategy. Refer to the above list when considering the following examples.

The Australian Ballet – Body & Soul campaign

Recently the Australian Ballet created a promotional campaign that attempted to expand the appeal of the ballet beyond its older demographic. The 're-positioning' of the ballet was built around a brand concept called Body & Soul. Patrick McIntyre, Australian Ballet Communications Manager stated: '...in common with many arts organisations, the Australian Ballet seeks to encourage younger audiences while continuing to satisfy and respect its existing supporters. This presents a number of challenges and complexities in the way in which we shape our communications and marketing materials.'

McIntyre went on to say that their recent Body & Soul campaign '...presented a contemporary and appealing image without appearing flashy, desperate and faddish. It [the campaign] was respectful of the company's historical representation and positioning ... and reinforced the notions of 'dance' as a physical, energetic, sexy and accessible medium'. [5]

Starbucks

Starbucks state their mission to be the "premier purveyor of the finest coffee". Additionally, the essential promise of the brand and the in-store experience is one of community, camaraderie and connection.[6]

Petrol Records

City Series compilations – 'The Sex. The City. The Music ...will romance and dance you through the hottest and most happening cities in the world. ... A time to ignite your musical senses – a time to replenish your musical collection.'[7]

QANTAS – New international business class seating

"It's all about new levels of comfort – it's all about you."[8]

Audi A3

"Be Consumed – Drive the new Audi A3 and you will be consumed." [9]

Dick Smith Foods

Australian food processor Dick Smith uses patriotism to differentiate his grocery products by stressing that they are all Australian grown and manufactured.

Positioning strategy for music and musicians

Applying conventional marketing concepts to creative artists is fraught with complexity. Imagine a manager asking a band the following question:

Manager: 'How do you see your value proposition positioned in the pop market?'
The band: 'Huh?'

The manager might be better served by approaching positioning strategy by describing it as **developing a distinctive image**. This is not to insult the band's intelligence – only that the approach to band management needs to be less academic and more rock'n'roll.

The success of pop/rock music relies on renewal. New artists, new music, new songs, new attitudes. New implies different – implies differentiation. This is the essence of market positioning. Being different, being cool, creating a new sound, look or image are goals of both artists and consumer product manufactures. Consider the following examples of how rock bands position or develop a distinctive image in the minds of music consumers.

The Darkness

These British rockers certainly have a distinctive look and sound and in recent times have been one the most talked-about rock bands in the world. They have re-invented 70's glam-rock, bringing style, attitude, camp showmanship (and the guitar solo) back to rock – elements that were cast aside by a decade of Nirvana/Pearl Jam inspired introspective rockers.

Jet

Jet rock like there's no tomorrow, yet they also roll like the greats of yesterday. As their debut album *Get Born* proves, this Melbourne four piece, Nic Cester (guitar/vocals), Chris Cester (drums/vocals), Cameron Muncey (guitar/vocals), Mark Wilson (bass), stand for everything that is raw, primitive, direct and loose about rock music. Jet bring with them a lucidity and freshness that comes from both youth and sheer Oz-centric bloodymindedness. Jet don't know the rules, and even if they did, they'd break them.[10]

Velvet Revolver

Velvet Revolver is everything the band's name suggests and much more. This is modern rock with a sense of danger and beauty that's been missing for far too long. Their suitably explosive yet gorgeous debut effort, *Contraband*, marks the spot for a new beginning from a band of rock & roll brothers united by some legendary pasts and a suddenly brighter future. Positioned as a super group, Velvet Revolver brings together three former members of one of rock's greatest groups, Guns N' Roses — Slash, bassist Duff McKagan and drummer Matt Sorum — with one of rock's most charismatic frontmen, Scott Weiland, formerly of Stone Temple Pilots, and guitarist Dave Kushner, ex-Wasted Youth, Electric Love Hogs and Dave Navarro's [Jane's Addiction] band, among others. [11]

Brands and brand strategy

What are brands?

A brand as defined by the American Marketing Association is "a name, term, design, symbol, or any other feature that identifies one seller's good or service as distinct from those of other sellers."[12]

Brands are not just logos

Building a successful brand is not just thinking of a clever name and designing some cool artwork. **Brand equity** is the trust (or goodwill) that consumers place in a brand. It is not created quickly, or cheaply. Creating a new brand means **creating value through trust**, where none existed before.

While trust in brands was traditionally developed by providing quality, service and value, many marketers wrongly believe that a quality product combined with the right logo and mass advertising campaign will result in brand equity. Brands such as iPod, Microsoft, Fender, The Wiggles, BMW, Sony PSP are not just logos, they are quality products that capture the imagination of consumers and, consequently, define the standards for their product category.

Brand personality

Historically, brands were used to build trust between sellers and buyers, making it easier for consumers to make purchase decisions. In recent times brand strategists have attributed to brands, intangible human characteristics. No longer just indicators of quality and trust, brands now have personality, promise, purpose, philosophy and vision. The brand has evolved from a simple marker of quality to what advertising guru, Kevin Roberts describes as a "lovemark – or brands that inspire loyalty beyond reason"[13]

Brand communities

Brand communities are non-geographically bound communities, based on a structured set of social relationships among admirers of a brand and they exhibit three traditional markers of community: shared consciousness, rituals and traditions, and a sense of moral responsibility.[14]

There are many notable examples often cited, including: Harley Davidson, Saab, Star Wars, Star Trek, Apple, Oracle, Virgin, Jeep (Chrysler), MySpace and blogs in general. Such examples share in part the experience of successful bands, who are able to create fierce brand loyalty amongst their fans.

Marketing highlight – Marketing cool

'Cool' is a personal thing. One person might say that Justin Timberlake is cool, while another might say that Sepultura are cool. Cool is an attitude – trying to be cool is un-cool. Cool brands (like bands) have personality, authentic attitude and are rebellious. Cool brands are almost impossible to contrive and seem often appear more by accident than design - the magic of coolness is the mystery that surrounds it.

While young consumers are desperate to be seen as cool they are repelled by "try-hards". When attempting to manufacture cool, note Louis Armstrong's alleged response when someone asked him what jazz was: "If you have to ask, you'll never know".[15]

Study Questions
1   Is cool an invention of marketing and media, or does it emerge and evolve on its own terms?
2   How do you make a product cool?
3   Are there cool 'things', ideas and concepts that are free of commercialisation? List and critique.

Brand names

Developing distinct, effective brand names can be difficult. Like a pop-song melody, brand names (and band names) must **hook** the mind of the prospective consumer. They must be unique and they must seek to engage the target audience with compelling links to product benefits. Brand names come in a number of varieties.

Brand Type	Description	Examples
Descriptive and associative	Brand names that: Describe the function of the product or service. Hint at an aspect or benefit of the product/ service offering. Express their market positioning.	Opera Australia Musicmax Windex Head & Shoulders shampoo 3 - 3rd generation mobile technology No Sweat – deodorant by Revlon the biz – music business marketing
Stand alone	Brand names that have no tangible link to the product, but may (or may not) have meaning of their own. Try coining a phrase – made up words are less likely to already be in use.	Apple Computer – the fruit of the same name bears no relationship to computer products. Kodak – a word invented by its founder George Eastman Zomba, Compaq, Fructis, Zendorphin, Filmtasm, Waxusic.

Company and/or family names	Commonly used by organisations whose brand names were derived from the person who first invented or developed the product.	Ford motor car company (founded by Henry Ford) Warner Music Australia Bang and Olufsen
Acronyms	An acronym is a word that is formed from the initial letters of the original brand or company name. Although acronym brands do sound conservative, some bands have used them in a clever, ironic and memorable way. Acronyms often become brands unto themselves, with consumers often forgetting or disregarding the original name.	ABBA – initial letters of the 4 band members' names REM – Rapid Eye Movement ELO – Electric Light Orchestra POD – Payable on Death BMG – Bertelsmann Music Group MTV – Music Television DKNY – Donna Karen New York KFC – Kentucky Fried Chicken AMP – Australian Mutual Provident

Case Study– MySpace: the ultimate brand community?

Within the MySpace environment we see a perfect example of the young generations redefining their communities, based on their terms, within their native environment – the digital world.

This combination of technology and their the timeless desire for community has rocketed MySpace to the top of U.S. web site traffic, accounting for 4.46 percent of all U.S. Internet visits for the week ending July 8 2006. This has pushed it past Yahoo Mail for the first time and it outpaces the home pages for Yahoo, Google and Microsoft's MSN Hotmail. MySpace, which dominates social networking on the Web, also gained share in June (2006) from other sites that aim to create virtual communities online for sharing music, photos or other interests.[16]

Gayle Troberman, MSN director of branded entertainment and experiences, explains MySpace's appeal: "This medium's incredibly personal. Experience is nonlinear and participatory. If you want an emotional connection, there's no better way to do that than by letting the consumer actually shape or be part of that experience. The powerful thing we've seen is the idea of community. There's me and my friends and my peer group.[17]

Be it an online community, social network, brand community or just a place for friends to hang out, MySpace has proven (in the case of UK band Arctic Monkeys) to be an exceptional music marketing tool.

Study Questions
1. Search the Internet for the Arctic Monkeys
2. What role has MySpace played in their rise up the 2006 UK single charts?
3. What lessons can be learnt from their use of MySpace?
4. Will MySpace continue to dominate youth online communities? What other alternatives are there to MySpace?
5. What ethical questions should marketers consider when using an online community as a marketing resource?

marketing plan builder

Marketing Plan Builder

Use the Marketing Plan Builder template to develop your music marketing plan. At the conclusion of each chapter the Builder will add a new section to assist in the planning process.

Stage four: Developing a product offering

Once you have defined your target market and established the existence of an unmet need, you must now refine your initial product/service concept. Earlier in the planning process you probably conceived a product – now is the time to develop it so that it truly matches the needs and desires of your selected market.

Describe the basic elements of your product?

_____

_____

What are the core (intangible) benefits your customers are seeking?

_____

_____

List five words that describe how customers will perceive your product.

_____

_____

List the physical components, shapes, colours, sizes, models, or – in the case of bands –their style, image, music and songs.

_____

_____

What augmented (or additional) services, warranty, credit facilities,

loyalty or membership programs might you offer customers?

_____

_____

thebiz – music business portal

www.thebiz.com.au
Download digital version of the Marketing Plan Builder

Study questions

1   How do products differ from services?
2   What is the relevance of experiences as a component of a product strategy?
3   What are the elements of a music business value proposition?
4   Are product life cycle graphs effective in predicting future sales performance of music products?
5   Define product positioning.
6   Why is it important for music businesses to have a unique selling proposition?
7   What are **brands**, and why has their role seemingly increased in importance?
8   Are bands brands? What are the advantages and disadvantages of regarding artists as commercial 'products'?
9   What is a brand community? Why might they effective in generating brand loyalty?

Chapter Five

PRICING & DISTRIBUTING MUSIC PRODUCTS

Learning outcomes

By the end of this chapter you should be able to:
- describe the process of setting prices for music products
- define pricing strategy and tactics
- identify distribution strategies used by artists and record labels
- define distribution and channel management tactics.

Price setting for music products and services

Setting prices is a critical step in the development of a coherent marketing mix. Set your prices too high and customers won't be able to afford your products. Set prices too low, and they will think that your products are poor quality and not worth buying.

Clearly your profit margin must be large enough for the product or project to be viable. Breaking even (where sales = expenses) is not enough; profits must be made. Setting prices involves a number of steps, which we shall explore. Special attention will be given to how CD prices are set by record labels as well as the price-setting process for live events.

A pricing strategy has several purposes.
- To establish the price-to-quality ratio that prospective consumers will use to judge the relative value of your product/service.
- To set pricing objectives.
- To create a profile of anticipated demand for the product/service.
- To establish cost structures of value propositions allowing the setting of profitable prices.
- To determine break-even point – the point at which sales are equal to expenses.
- To determine the pricing strategies and tactics of competitors and industry price points.
- To establish promotional pricing tactics such as discounts and introductory pricing.

Set pricing-to-quality strategy

We have seen in earlier chapters the critical role **positioning** plays in the creation of a new value proposition. Consumers use price as a measure of quality, thus the balance between the product quality and price is crucial if the value proposition is to be correctly positioning in consumers' minds.

While conventional marketing practice, and anecdotal evidence, points to the strong link between price and quality, applying it to an artist is difficult. While it is possible to compare the product quality of one brand of toaster to another, comparing musical artists or bands depends on individual tastes. It is completely subjective. A typical opera buff for example, may not believe Metallica is quality and a Green Day fan may not think The Wiggles are quality – when in fact they all create quality music/entertainment experiences relative to the tastes of their fan bases.

The following table contrasts the pricing strategies of intangible and tangible music-related products. It highlights how it is relatively simple to apply conventional pricing strategy to a product like a Fender Stratocaster guitar, while it is far more difficult to apply it to concert ticket prices. Note that the examples of premium product price strategy are straight forward – high price means high quality. The cheaper strategies, however, prove that while they might be useful for measuring toasters, cars or guitars, you cannot infer that because an artist charges a low price that they are low quality. It is far too judgmental and impractical from a management perspective to say that because Neil Diamond, Jack Johnson or Machine Gun Fellatio, for example, are lower cost they are therefore lower quality.

Contrasting pricing strategies applied to physical consumer goods and intangible entertainment products

		Tangible Product		Intangible Experience	
Price strategy	Definition	Fender Stratocaster guitars	Price $AUD	Artist	Ticket prices $AUD
Super premium	High-margin high quality (or perceived high quality) prestige brands	Fender Strat 62 Reissue	$3799	Barbara Streisand	Front row seats $1500
Premium	High quality high price products & services	Fender 50th Anniversary Stratocaster	$2549	The Eagles	Front row seats $560
High value	Medium price with high quality	Fender Strat Highway	$1799	Neil Diamond	All seats $100
Medium value	Medium quality – medium price	Mexican Stratocaster	$999	Jack Johnson*	$15–50
Economy	Low quality – low price	Affinity Series Strat	$699	Machine Gun Fellatio*	$20

* The authors are not implying that either Jack Johnson or Machine Gun Fellatio are low quality because their concert tickets are lower in price, only that conventional pricing strategies can be difficult to apply when dealing with subjective product quality.

Pricing objectives

Cost-plus pricing

Perhaps the most common method of pricing products is cost-plus, meaning that you add a percentage (or margin) to the total cost of producing a product. The margin you select will either allow you to break even, or to reach an arbitrarily determined profit figure.

Survival pricing

Companies desperate to stay afloat use survival pricing strategy, which is clearly not a desirable situation for a firm. This strategy involves heavy price discounting, which although may halt imminent financial disaster, results in damage to brand equity. When stock is sold off cheaply, people may begin to think the products are cheap quality.

Market skimming (price skimming)

Market, or price skimming is where prices are set high to take advantage of strong demand for new or highly desirable events or products. It is common for concert promoters to charge high prices for shows in venues they know will easily sell out. This ensures that the profit margin per ticket is maximised and that there are no empty seats. The Rolling Stones appearing at Sydney's relatively small Enmore theatre comes to mind. Think also of major one-off events where demand for tickets far exceeds the venue capacity, say the Olympics closing ceremony or the World Cup football final.

Market penetration – maximum market share

In this case prices are set low to maximise sales and therefore market share. It is assumed, however, that such a strategy implies the product/service does not have a premium market position. You simply cannot charge low prices for products that have a high perceived or actual quality. Premium buyers such as the AB demographic (see Chapter 3) will not accept that quality comes cheap.

Price penetration, therefore, is best suited to highly competitive markets where product quality is important but not premium in nature and market share leadership is the prize. The computer game console market and the market share battle between Sony Playstation, X-Box and Nintendo Game Cube. In this market, manufacturers take advantage of the desire of hard-core gamers to pay higher prices for the latest technology.

Product-service quality leadership

Quality leaders assume the premium or super-premium pricing strategy. Their products have a high level of actual or perceived quality and their consumers are prepared to pay high prices for the highest quality. Entertainment equipment manufacturers Bang and Olufsen and Bose are good examples, as are many products and services that target wealthier demographic groups. Barbara Streisand's last tour to Australia is also a example of premium pricing, where the best seats where priced at $1500.

Estimate demand

Estimating demand is the most difficult stage in setting prices as it involves prediction. How do we know how many CDs, concert tickets or merchandise items we will sell? Since we cannot predict the future, we need to make an educated guess. Existing companies are able to make more accurate predictions of demand because they have a history. They draw on past successes and failures for inspiration. Start up businesses do not have that luxury. As a band, if you are about to have your CD pressed, how many copies do you order? How many will you sell?

Some simple demand estimating techniques

- Monitor the mainstream and independent music charts and note the sales volume of bands similar to yours.
- Network – get to know other bands, their managers and other industry insiders who can assist you in determining potential demand for your product.
- Study economic modelling concepts – although beyond the scope of this text, the study of the economics of supply and demand can assist you in determining future sales volume.
- Market research – primary and secondary research techniques will assist you in developing a picture of market demand (see Chapter 2).

Estimate costs and break-even points

Unlike estimating demand, estimating costs is one element in price setting that is not realm of the fortune-teller. The costs associated with recording and manufacturing CDs and costing merchandise and live events can be readily established.

In order to effectively determine the costs and therefore the break-even point we need to analyse the two categories of costs.

Fixed costs

Fixed costs, or overheads as they are commonly referred to, are those costs that remain constant regardless of the number of products you sell or manufacture. They include such costs as electricity, rent, insurance and permanent staff. If you owned a CD store, for example, the rent on your retail space remains the same, regardless of whether you sell ten CDs or thousands.

Variable costs

Variable costs are those that vary with the level of sales and/or production. Variable costs for the CD store include casual staff wages and the stock CDs available for sale. Take the casual staff for example; if the store suddenly experiences a rush on CDs then the store manager might have to put on more staff to handle increasing demand. Also, the store manager might be able to negotiate quantity discounts from the record distributor, as larger shipments mean cheaper cost per unit on the CDs.

A demonstration of cost-plus pricing

As mentioned earlier, a simple way of determining price is to add a percentage mark-up to the overall cost of producing a product. We need, therefore, to establish the unit cost of producing each item to then add a mark-up. Suppose you plan to produce t-shirts on behalf of bands in your local area and have established the following costs:

Variable cost = cost of the t-shirts, the ink and the packaging material.
Fixed costs = the total costs associated with the running your business, including your screen-printing facility, studio rental, electricity, office equipment and insurance.
Expected sales = the number of t-shirts you expect to sell.

Variable cost per unit   = $8
Fixed cost   = $40,000
Expected sales   =   5000

Equation:

$$\text{unit cost} \; = \; \text{variable cost} \; + \left(\frac{\text{fixed cost}}{\text{expected sales}} \right) \; = \; \$8 \; + \left(\frac{\$40,000}{5000} \right) \; = \; \$16$$

Mark-up – Let us assume that you would like to sell your t-shirts for $20 each. This would represent a 20% mark-up on the $16 unit cost.

Determining break-even points

You now wish to know how many t-shirts you need to sell in order to break even. This can be determined using the following formula:

$$\text{Breakeven volume} \; = \; \frac{\text{fixed cost}}{\text{price} - \text{variable cost}} \; = \; \frac{\$40,000}{\$20 - \$16} \; = \; 10000 \text{ units}$$

Break-even sales ($) = break-even volume x   mark-up
                       = 10000 x $20 = $200,000

Production budgets

Available on **thebiz.com.au** are an extensive range of production budgets that will assist you in determining cost, break-even and profitability for music business ventures. They include:

- gig budget (single show)
- tour budget (multiple shows)
- festival / event budget
- cash flow forecast – manager/agent business
- cash flow forecast – record label
- Australian publishing royalty calculator
- foreign sub-publishing royalty calculator
- musical equipment depreciation calculator
- CD production budget and price breakdown
- break-even analysis – single merchandise product
- multi-product break-even analysis – merchandise

thebiz – music business portal
www.thebiz.com.au
Download CD, event and merchandise break-even calculators

Assess competitor pricing strategies

Price points

The record business, like many industries, is one where prices are relatively static, meaning that there are well-established price points for the various music formats such as CDs, DVDs, mp3 etc. It is critical, therefore, that when establishing prices for your products you consider industry benchmarks. This is not to say that you shouldn't attempt to try new innovative pricing models, after all, the mp3 revolution created the ultimate price point breaker – the free (if illegal) download. The following table shows some retail price points as at October 2006.

Format price points (recommended retail prices)

Format	High price point	Medium price point	Low price point
CD album (1 CD)	$33.00	$24.95	$9.95
CD & DVD set	$48.00	$33	$24.95
Vinyl album	$33.50	$28.00	$15.95
DVD music video	$35.00	$19.95	$12.95
SCAD (super audio CD)	$56.00	$44.00	$27.00
mp3 per track	$1.87	$0.99	$0.49
Ring tone (original recording)	$6.60	$4.40	$2.20

Pricing tactics and terminology

Cash discounts – Despite the prevalence of credit cards and electronic banking (EFTPOS), cash discounts still count.

Credit – Credit is used by retailers to encourage purchase. It is not uncommon today for large retailers to sell goods on credit and allow their customers to repay over several years, interest free.

Flexible payment terms – When retailers purchase CDs from a record distributor that pays on account, this means they take delivery of the goods and agree to pay later. The record distributor then offers discounts off the invoice amount if the retailer pays earlier than expected.

Loss-leader pricing – A promotional pricing strategy where seller sets a very low price, at cost or below cost, to attract customers and entice them to buy other products in addition (or instead of) their loss-leader purchase.

P.P.D. – Published Price to Dealer – used by the record and music publishing industry to describe wholesale price of music products and sheet music.

Quantity discounts – As discussed earlier, this is a tried and true method of sales promotional pricing.

R.R.P. – Recommended Retail Price – recommended by the manufacturer to the retailer.

Soft pricing – Where a CD is priced at $24.95 rather than $25 to soften the blow. It's an old (obvious) tactic, but we all fall for it.

Warranties – Free or low cost warranties are considered a pricing tactic in that they add value to a product.

Distribution

Definition

Distribution refers to the set of people, organisations and places involved in providing access to your products and services. These channels of distribution must be designed to meet both the needs and expectations of consumers as well as satisfy company objectives. They must be consistent with the market positioning strategy to ensure consistent branding.

It should be noted that distribution theory and practice is most often applicable to physical products. Services with their intangibility (see Chapter 4) often involve no middlemen or intermediaries between manufacturer and consumer, making distribution strategy seem redundant.

Intermediaries – participants in distribution

Intermediaries, often referred to as **channel partners**, play a crucial role in providing points of access for consumers seeking your products. They include:

- **Manufacturers:** for the purposes of our study we shall refer to artists/bands as manufacturers who supply their product (recordings) to record labels, who are regarded as wholesalers.
- **Wholesalers:** are companies that purchase products from several manufacturers and on-sell them to retailers.
- **Retailers:** provide public access to a range or products.
- **Agents:** act on behalf of a manufacturer but importantly, do not take title (legal ownership) of the products. They then typically take commission (or percentage) of the sale price of the goods.

The role of record labels in distribution

Record labels are the manufacturers and wholesalers of music product. Historically, they have been unwilling to enter the retail arena because:

1. they have well-established allegiances with retail partners.
2. labels themselves are not consumer brands. Consumers recognise Sanity, HMV, Virgin Megastore, Tower Records as CD retailing brands – not Bertelsmann Media Group (BMG) and Universal Music Australia Ltd.

The music distribution landscape, however, has changed. Labels, and their artists, can effectively promote directly to consumers and sell product via the web. Music retailers are already changing their focus from CDs to DVDs and consumer electronics.

Simultaneously, record labels are beginning to compete with their retail partners. Conceivably, they could sell digital music far cheaper than the equivalent CD. See **www.thebiz.com.au** to learn more.

Before examining the various types of distribution set-ups in the recording industry, let's consider some key terminology:

Digital distribution – is the downloading of music as a digital file (mp3, WMA etc) that is stored on disc or portable playback device. Digital distribution also includes streaming audio such as is offered by Real Networks – although the war between downloading verses streaming is all but over. Downloads have won. Digital distribution can also include the transfer of digital music files to PDAs (portable data assistants) and mobile phones, where they are typically used as ring tones.

In-store CD sales – compact discs bought in the old fashioned 'bricks and mortar' store.

Location CD sales – compact discs sold by the artist/band directly to the public at live events and on tour.

Online CD sales – compact discs paid for over the internet and delivered by post or courier to customers.

Methods of distributing music product

Consider the following classic distribution scenarios used to deliver music product to consumers.

Independent band/artist without CD distribution deal

Band / Artist	How is this achieved?	
↓	Internet distribution CD sales at shows/gigs Mail order sales	
	Advantages	**Advantages**
Consumers / Fans	Higher per unit profit margin than other methods. Creative control over all aspects of promotion.	You have to cover all costs of promotion and distribution. Limited access to media, retail and industry networks.

Artist is signed directly to record company

Band / Artist	**How is this achieved?**	
↓	This is the classic record contract scenario. An artist creates master recordings which the label owns and then markets.	
	Advantages (for artist)	Disadvantages (for artist)
Record label	Record company pays for artist's fame.	Lower per unit profit margin.
↓	Label is responsible for all aspects of promotion.	Less creative freedom than other types of recording deals.
Retailer	Wide market coverage and access to nationwide music retailers.	Label owns the master recording.
↓	Label arranges in-store promotion and dealer incentives for retailers. Label also stimulates demand by promoting directly to consumers.	CD sales may not be enough for the label to recoup the money it spent recording the masters (also called recording advances).
Consumers /Fans	Label may provide funding support for the artist to tour. Record label A&R (Artist and Repertoire) support and development.	

Artist with independent recording and distribution deals

Artist/Indie label	How is this achieved?
 Independent record distributor  Retailer ↓ Consumers / Fans	The **John Butler Trio** is the classic case study here. John Butler co-owns independent label, Jarrah Records, which produces his albums, and those of **The Waifs**. In turn, these albums are distributed by MGM Distribution via a P&D (pressing and distribution) deal.

	Advantages (for Artist)	Disadvantages (to Artist)
	Distributor is responsible for pushing product through the distribution channel.	Artist/Indie label is responsible for promotion to radio and fans.
	Higher profit margin than in a direct signing deal with a major label.	Artist lacks the record label promotional budget and, importantly, misses out on tour support (funding that in part subsidises tours).
	Wide market coverage – access to nationwide music retailers. This is very useful in combination with national triple J airplay. Fans can walk into their local record store anywhere in Australia and order your CD.	Artist lacks the major record label media contacts. Artist lacks major record label A&R (artist and repertoire) support and development.
	The Indie owns the master recordings – this is great if you are the Indie!	

Major record label distribution scenario

The following diagram demonstrates the basic elements of a major record label distribution system. Sony/BMG weave both online and offline distribution scenarios that for example, delivers Delta Goodrem CDs, DVDs, mp3, WMA files and mobile phone ring tones to customers.

Major label record distribution

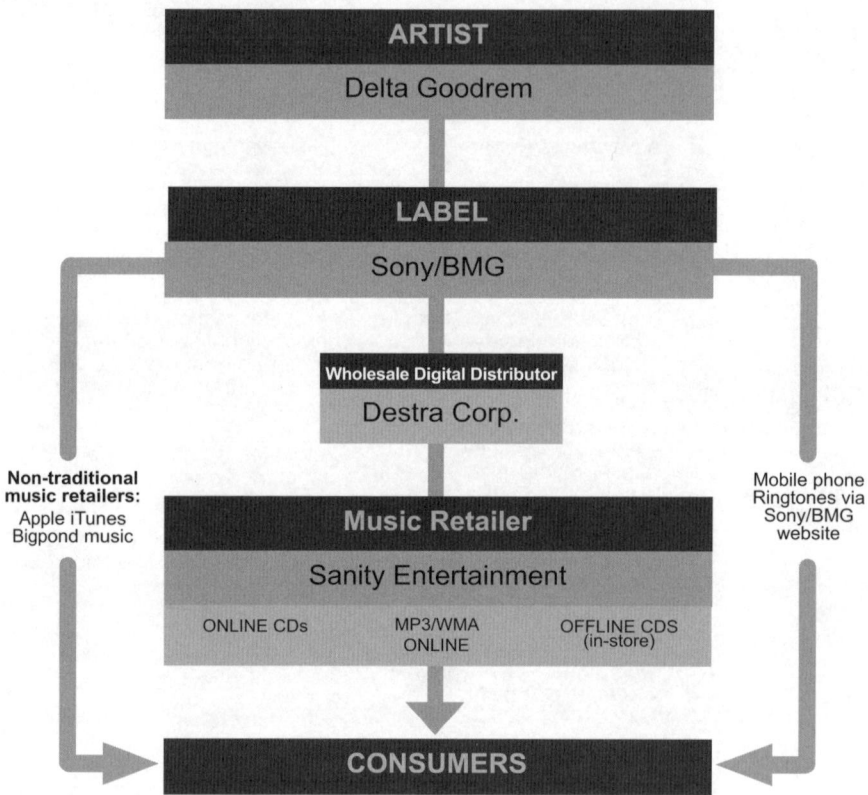

Digital Rights Managers

Companies such as Destra Corporation are in the business of securing digital distribution licences from record companies. Then they provide online mp3 sales systems for third parties, such as Sanity Entertainment and JB HiFi. These online/offline retailers then sell the mp3 alongside CDs, DVDs and other merchandise supplied by the artist/label.

Can 'bricks and mortar' compete?

As mentioned earlier, record companies have comfortable strategic retailing partnerships with record stores. Given that Sony/BMG, for example, already sells mobile phone ring tones online, how long will it be before they challenge 'bricks and mortar' music retailers such as Sanity. How long before they sell mp3 directly from their website and eliminate the middlemen altogether?

Providing channel incentives

Trade oriented sales promotion

Trade oriented sales promotion targets the distribution and retail channel partners, encouraging them to stock and then actively promote the products either to retail customers, or to other members of the channel. It is also known as a **push strategy** since it attempts to force the channel to give customers access to products.

The role of trade oriented sales promotion has become increasingly important due to:

- Most markets (including music markets) are filled with competing, often similar, products, meaning that differentiated offerings are difficult to create.
- The Australian music-retailing environment is dominated by a handful of large retail chains that exert considerable power over the (wholesaling) record companies and their distributors.
- The limited availably of shelf space allows the retailers to demand greater in-store promotion at the record label's expense.
- The diminished power of mass media advertising to 'pull' demand through the channel.
- The availability of retail sales data via barcode scanners and other technology that increases measurability. This places pressure on the record companies and distributors to perform since retailers can accurately measure sales in relation to in-store promotion.
- Recent changes to the Copyright Act permitting parallel importation allows retailers to source low cost (legitimate) CDs from overseas forcing downward pressure on local PPDs. (the term used by record companies for the wholesale price of a CD).

The other variety, **consumer oriented sales promotion**, is designed to encourage, compel and even cajole retail shoppers into making immediate purchase decisions. It is often referred to as the **pull approach**. More on consumer sales promotion in Chapter 8.

Sales promotion and CD retailing

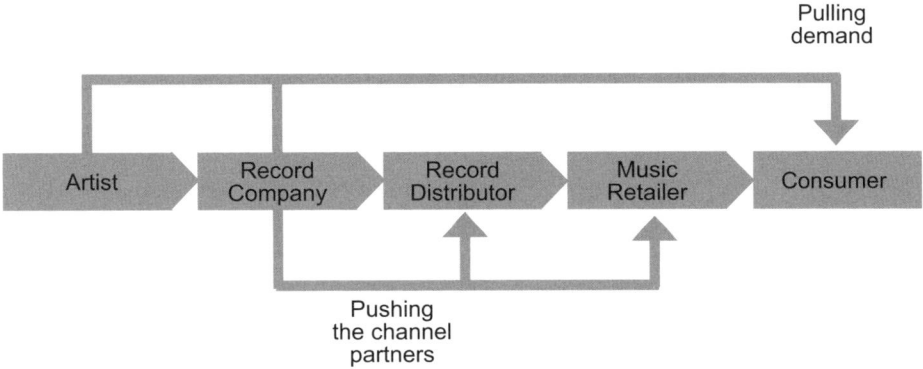

Trade promotion strategies

Point-of-sale merchandising and demonstration

- posters
- product displays
- end-of-aisle bins, product stands and displays
- listening posts, where shoppers sample a selection of CDs

In-store artist appearances

- in-store CD signings
- in-store performances

Free goods and price discounts

- Free merchandise, such as t-shirts and sampler CDs, given to retail management and staff within record stores.
- The baker's dozen principle, where retailers are given free additional products (they can sell) if they order a certain number of products.
- Given increasing retailer power, record and distribution companies are increasingly willing to be flexible on their PPD.

Marketing Plan Builder

Use the Marketing Plan Builder template to develop your music marketing plan. At the conclusion of each chapter the Builder will add a new section to assist in the planning process.

Stage five: Developing pricing and distribution

Having designed your value proposition in the previous plan builder, it is now time to consider what pricing strategy and distribution model you will use.

Describe your preferred distribution method (DIY, Indie label deal etc).

_____

_____

Choose a pricing strategy that best matches your target audience's perceptions of value and their capacity to pay.

_____

_____

Visit **thebiz.com.au** and download a cost calculator appropriate to your music project. Customise the calculator and generate a pricing model.

_____

_____

Assess competitor prices and industry price points and adjust your price accordingly.

_____

_____

Develop promotional pricing tactics to encourage adoption of the value proposition by both retailers and customers where appropriate.

_____

_____

○ ○ ○   thebiz - music business portal

www.thebiz.com.au
Download digital version of the
Marketing Plan Builder

marketing plan builder

Study questions

1   Describe the link between product quality and price. What role does it play in setting prices for entertainment events and music products?

2   What are the major considerations when setting prices for products?

3   What is the difference between pricing strategy and pricing tactics?

4   What is a price point? Under what circumstances should you be guided by price points and when should you ignore them?

5   How important is access to music retailers for independent musicians?

6   Can Indie labels and artists use the internet to by-pass traditional retailers? How realistic a proposition is this?

7   What are the advantages of remaining independent?

8   What are the distribution advantages in signing a major recording or distribution contract?

9   Describe push and pull sales promotion tactics?

10 What role does promotional pricing play in encouraging retailers to actively promote your product in-store?

Chapter Six

INTRODUCTION TO INTEGRATED MARKETING COMMUNICATION

Learning outcomes

By the end of this chapter you should be able to:
- define the promotional mix
- develop an integrated marketing communications strategy for music products
- design a campaign strategy for music products.

The marketing communication process

As discussed earlier, an effective marketing strategy is built upon a deep appreciation of the needs and expectations of consumers. Market segments and their buying characteristics must be tracked and measured. Entertainment products, services and experiences are then designed to meet the core emotional needs of the consumers.

In light of this, successful entertainment promotional campaigns do not seek to tell people what they should buy; rather they make emotional connections with market segments and their purchase aspirations. They communicate product benefits and lead consumers to enjoyable and rewarding purchase experiences.

Don't fall into the trap of believing 'that if I spend enough money telling people they should buy a product, they will'. This common yet simplistic view of marketing communications will likely lead to poor results.

The promotional mix – an integrated approach

The promotional 'P' is often the most visible component of the marketing mix, since it incorporates the advertising and promotional elements. It is not, however, as many believe, the single most important aspect of a marketing plan. Remember also that the terms **promotion** and **advertising** are not substitute terms for marketing. Rather, the promotional mix serves to connect buyers to the value proposition and should be designed to convey the benefits of ownership.

Integrated marketing communication (IMC)

Integrated marketing communications (IMC) refers to the strategic coordination of all forms of communication between a product or firm its target markets. The purpose of IMC is to ensure that no one element of the promotional mix (advertising, publicity, public relations, sales-promotion, direct marketing, sales) is executed without considering its impact on all other elements in the promotional mix. It is a coordinated and integrated approach to marketing communications.

Why IMC and not just a promotional mix?

There are several reasons for the increasing adoption of IMC by marketers. They are:

1. Treating the complex task of communication as just another one of the four Ps does not satisfactorily address the critical importance of integrating messages across the promotional mix elements. A one-dimensional approach also doesn't assist in developing a consistent, integrated company-wide approach to communicating with the outside world.
2. Media fragmentation – in recent years there has been massive proliferation in the types of media that consumers use to access information and be entertained.
3. Because of media fragmentation, micro-segment targeting has developed, which requires tighter integration with other elements of the promotional mix.
4. The declining impact of mass media advertising. With media fragmentation comes the diminishing role of television advertising. Audiences are watching less television than before and the dominant role of advertising agents (who traditionally favour mass media advertising) is being usurped by integrated approaches that do not favour one media form over another.
5. New media – the Internet, e-marketing, virtual communities, gaming, mobile messaging, mobile computing, PDAs and cable television are relative newcomers. Combining these new technologies with traditional forms of promotion requires tight integration.
6. The rise of metrics – measuring the effects of mass media advertising on sales is problematic. Not so with new media. Website traffic and opt-ins to SMS promotions can be measured objectively and budgets justified.

Demonstrated on the following page is a flow chart that links the marketing plan to the integrated marketing communications plan.

Integrated marketing communications planning

This is designed to explain each stage of the integrated marketing communications planning process shown on the following page. It is helpful to think of the diagram as a table of contents that would appear in a written IMC plan.

IMC situation analysis

The purpose of the IMC situation analysis is to summarise issues arising from the marketing plan that will directly impact on the communications strategy. Do not re-write the marketing plan; rather draw from it the following items:

Company analysis

- company mission
- corporate goals
- issues related to an overriding corporate brand (if one exists)
- budget for the IMC

Integrated marketing communications planning

Strategic Marketing Plan

Integrated Marketing Communications (IMC) Plan

IMC Situation Analysis

Company Analysis	Product Analysis	Audience Analysis	Competitor Campaigns

Communication Objectives

Awareness	Preference	Stimulate Sales

Strategic Communications Plan

Campaign Impact & Duration	Creative Strategy	Integration Strategies	Promotional Budget

Promotional Mix

Advertising Strategy	Public Relations Strategy	Direct Marketing Strategy	Sales Promotion Strategy	Sales Force Strategy	Sponsor-ship & Events	Packaging

Implementation

Project Timeline	Control Mechanisms	Measure Campaign Effectiveness (Metrics)

Product analysis

- a summary of key product offerings and product life cycle issues
- existing brand themes, messages and appeals

Audience analysis

- How closely do they align with the target markets?
- Are they the same people, or is there variance?
- What do they currently know about you?
- What media do they currently access most often?
- What is their degree of resistance to you?
- Are you trying to influence a negative attitude an audience has toward you?

Competitor campaigns

- Include an analysis of your competitors' communication objectives, target audiences, creative concepts and messages, media selection and promotional tactics.

Communication objectives

Communication objectives are often a source of confusion for marketers, many of whom point out that the objective of promotion and advertising is simply to sell products. That the ultimate goal of a marketing plan and its promotional activities is to *sell* is not in dispute. Sales volume is a marketing objective, not a communication objective. Consider the following example:

> A record company might set a marketing objective for a new pop release as: gold (50,000) CD sales over a 12 month period. The task of the IMC then is to translate this marketing objective into a communication objective that directs the specific communication tasks necessary to reach a stated sales figure.

Communication objectives, however, must be constructed to achieve goals that are not simply measured sales figures. Marketers who directly link sales performance with communication do so at their peril. If, for whatever reason, the product doesn't sell, the marketing department and its communication plan will receive the blame, even if there were other factors at work. Ultimately there can be a multitude of reasons for increases or decreases in sales, of which promotional campaigns are but one.

Communication objectives fall into three basic categories:

1. **Awareness** – to create or change levels of awareness in the target audience. This means you are either working from zero awareness, say for a new product or, alternatively, awareness exists and you wish to expand it. Typical communication objectives for awareness are:

   a. To create 40% awareness of *product x* in the target audience over the campaign period.
   b. To expand current awareness of *product y* from 40% to 60% awareness in the target audience over the campaign period.

2. **Preference** – to influence audience preferences for products and services. Examples include:

> To create 40% preference for *product x* amongst the target audience over the period of the campaign.

3. **To stimulate sales** – Contrary to earlier comments, there are occasions where communication objectives may need to be constructed to stimulate sales. Situations might include communication plans that are heavily weighted to sales promotion, which is a communication tactic directly linked to sales performance.

Hierarchy of effects model

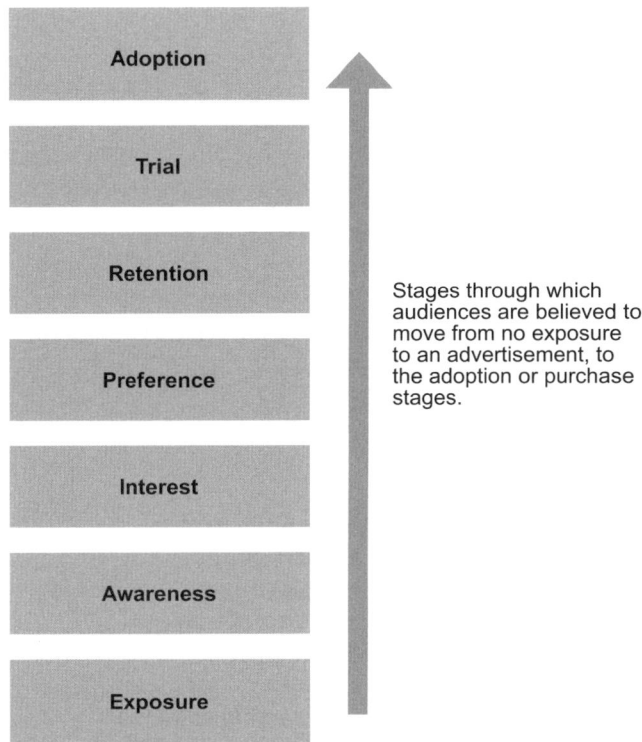

Adoption

Trial

Retention

Stages through which audiences are believed to move from no exposure to an advertisement, to the adoption or purchase stages.

Preference

Interest

Awareness

Exposure

Communications strategy

The communications strategy provides a broad framework by which to achieve the communication objectives. Strategic actions are developed by relating the communication objectives to the **IMC situation analysis**. Include the following:

Campaign impact and duration

- Is the strategy to **penetrate** the market rapidly?
- Or, will you try to build awareness and market share over a longer period of time?
- How long will the campaign last and what is the **timing** of each element?

Creative strategy

- develop an overall theme, appeal and message concept

Integration strategies

- Ensure that **brand personality** is embedded in all media.
- **Tangible links** between mix elements. There should be no isolated promotional items – all media must be linked, each one dependent on another.
- Think **touchpoints**, or moments in the day when your target audience experiences or accesses their preferred media.
- **Don't talk at them** – make your messages experiential (see Chapter Eight).
- Keep a **consistent 'look and feel'** across all design elements.
- Leverage of **cross-promotional tie-ins**.

Promotional budget

- Allocate budget for each promotional mix element.
- The proportion of the budget allocated to any one promotional element should reflect how accurately it reaches and impacts the target audience, relative to the other mix elements.

The promotional mix

While the elements of the promotional mix will be covered in detail in coming chapters, consider the following key components of each.

Advertising strategy
- advertising objectives
- media plan
- appeals and executions
- cost estimates

Public relations (PR) strategy
- PR objectives
- tactics and executions
- cost estimates

Direct marketing strategy
- DM objectives
- tactics and executions
- cost estimates

Sales promotion strategy
- sales promotion objectives
- tactics and executions
- cost estimates

Sales force strategy
- sales targets
- sales management tactics
- cost estimates

Sponsorship and events
- sponsorship objectives
- properties and events
- cost-benefit analysis

Packaging
- design and production
- cost estimates

Marketing highlight – common promotional mix objectives

Promotional element	Common objectives
Advertising	• To build brand awareness. • To build brand equity. • To drive attendance. • To drive sales. • To uphold image. • To inform and educate.
Public relations	• To inform, educate and engage the target audience and general public through the trusted medium of the press. • To generate critical support from influential journalists, critics and editors from targeted publications. • To generate x volume of 'column inches' of editorial in print publications. • To generate x volume of 'mentions' in the media. • To gain x volume of radio, TV and pay TV airplay for singles, album tracks and videos. • To secure on-air interviews with chosen television and radio programs.
Direct marketing & E-marketing	• To maintain high integrity database of customers and stakeholders. • x % response rate from conventional direct mail campaigns. • x % response rate from direct email campaigns. • To increase response rate from existing database of customers. • To increase website traffic by x %.
Sales promotion	• To provide incentive (to incentivise) customers after other mix elements lead prospective customers to the trial stage. • To facilitate product trial. • To generate ambient marketing collateral. • To increase street crew member. • To generate x volume of responses to competitions and special offers and coupons, in-store promotions and artist appearances. • To data-mine x number of prospects from competition entries.
Sales force strategy	• To build a CRM (customer relationship management) focus. • To solution sell – to partner with customers to solve their issues, rather than take their money and run. • To generate x number of sales leads. • To generate x volume of sales per day/week/month/quarter/ year. • To generate x volume of sales per market segment.
Sponsorship & events	• To generate x number of sponsors. • To generate x dollar value of sponsorship support. • To generate x dollar value contra sponsorship support (ie free or discounted advertising rates from media sponsors).

Implementation

Project timeline

Project timelines are like a calendar of events. Listed in priority order are all the tasks, elements and promotional executions set out in the communications strategy and promotional mix.

www.thebiz.com.au

Download a project management template that demonstrates a project timeline.

Control mechanisms

Once the campaign has been initiated it must be closely monitored and controlled. Part of this procedure is the use of metrics, but it is more than this. It is the role of a marketing-communication manager to ensure that all elements are correctly integrated and implemented.

Measuring campaign effectiveness (Metrics)

Integral to the IMC concept is **measurability**. Promotional campaigns and more specifically advertising, is often criticised for its lack of accountability. IMC on the other hand, presents an opportunity for music marketers to embrace accountability and provide tangible, justification for their existence – perhaps even increased budgets. While traditional advertising campaigns tended to focus on a few metrics such as audience share, the multifaceted IMC campaign requires a wide variety of metrics to deal with the many audience touchpoints. It's a case of careful what you wish for.

Thus, the purpose of **metrics**, or measurement tools, is to assess the cost-benefit of promotional campaigns. An example is the measurement of visitor numbers to your website following a newspaper advertisement displaying your domain name.

www.thebiz.com.au

Download a comprehensive integrated marketing communications planning template.

CASE STUDY – Setting IMC objectives & tactics for a CD release

A major record label plans to launch the debut album of its latest Oz-rock band. Six months prior to the scheduled release date, the label plans to begin building anticipation in the marketplace. The strategy is to release the first single (from the album) at the three-month mark. Once the album is released the label has set an objective of gold sales of 50,000 albums in the first year of release.

Duration	Objective	Promotional activities	Market size
Month 1	To expose 90% of the target audience to a minimum of three contacts with at least one element of promotional activity.	Teaser campaigns Simple messages Brand themes Create intrigue Launch website Showcase gigs for selected media and journalists Support shows with selected major artists	1 million teenagers
Month 2	Create 70% awareness of the brand/band among the target audience.	Descriptive copy adverts Media interviews	700,000 teenagers
Month 3	Create interest for the brand/band among 40% of the target audience	Release first single Commercial and non-commercial radio airplay Street crew activities begin	400,000 teenagers
Month 4	Create preference for the brand/band among 25% of the target audience.	Promotional & showcase gigs in state capitals Supported by radio/TV/press interviews In-store signings	250,000 teenagers
Month 5	Create message retention among 20% of the target audience.	Increase interviews, airplay &showcase gigs Competitions via web SMS and street crew activities	200,000 teenagers
Month 6	Create and maintain an established regular fan base among 5% of the target audience.	CD launch National tour begins Selected mass media advertisements	50,000 teenagers buy (Platinum album status)

marketing plan builder

Marketing Plan Builder

Use the Marketing Plan Builder template to develop your music marketing plan. At the conclusion of each chapter the Builder will add a new section to assist in the planning process.

Stage six: Structuring an integrated communication plan

Now we have established our value proposition, pricing and distribution strategy, it is time to consider how we will inform and educate our target market of the benefits of owning our products.

1   What is the overriding purpose of the communication plan? Is it to build brand awareness of a new product? Is it to increase brand awareness of an existing product that you are re-branding or repositioning?

_____

_____

2   What are the objectives of the overriding marketing? Are they to increase sales, market share or return on investment? How will you translate those objectives into clearly defined communication objectives, such as building brand awareness or brand preference?

_____

_____

3   How will you measure your objectives? As you move through the planning process you will discover that individual elements of the promotional mix can be assigned measurable objectives, like visitation numbers to measure a print advertisement that directs fans to a band website. Begin brainstorming possible ways to measure your campaign.

_____

_____

_____

_____

_____

_____

thebiz – music business portal

www.thebiz.com.au
Download digital version of the
Marketing Plan Builder

Study questions

1 Describe the concept of integrated marketing communications.

2 Why is it important to develop measurable objectives for promotional campaigns?

3 What is the difference between marketing, sales and a communication objective?

4 What are marketing metrics? Name three ways of measuring promotional campaign objectives?

5 Why should the elements of a promotional campaign be integrated?

6 What are the problems with attaching sales objectives to advertising?

7 Describe the stages in the **hierarchy of effects** model.

8 Why is it important to attach measurable objectives to each stage of the hierarchy of effects model?

Chapter Seven

DEVELOPING CREATIVE STRATEGY & MEDIA PLANNING

Learning outcomes

By the end of this chapter you should be able to:
- define creative strategy development
- develop a copy platform to brief an advertising agent
- evaluate media alternatives for an IMC
- develop a media plan.

Designing campaign themes and appeals

Any piece of promotional material must be created within the wider context of the integrated marketing communications and the marketing strategy that directs it. Campaign themes and appeal, therefore, must be created in the context of:
- marketing objectives
- communication objectives
- target audiences
- market positioning strategies
- product, service and brand strategy
- distribution and pricing.

Creative appeals

There are three types of appeals or approaches to designing an advertisement: rational, emotional and moral.

Rational

Rational appeals are those advertising messages that appeal to self-interest. They argue specific, tangible benefits of ownership. Quality, value, economy and performance benefits are stressed. Rational appeals are more common in business-to-business marketing situations where emotional arguments are less convincing.

Music industry example: If you are seeking event sponsorship from a clothing company you should make concise rational arguments as to why they should support you. This would include appeals that stress the economic benefits of being involved with an event whose target market corresponds with the sponsor's. You would also stress that sponsorship is a powerful alternative to traditional advertising, particularly in youth markets like music.

Emotional - experiential

Since the key driver of music consumption is the desire to be entertained, then obviously the majority of advertising appeals are emotional ones. Emotional appeals can be made both in a positive and a negative fashion. Clearly, in music, we would like to appeal to people with positive messages, rather than appealing to fear, guilt and shame, as do anti-smoking advertisements, for example.

Music industry example: Most video clips for rap, R&B and female pop artists incorporate sexual appeals. Clearly our innate sexual drives are exploited in the creative messages we receive from many artists and their marketing collateral.

Moral

Moral appeals are those advertising messages that appeal to our sense of what is right and wrong. Most moral appeals attempt to persuade us or to challenge our existing beliefs. While advertising messages can be reasonably successful in affecting people's attitudes to *brand x* verses *brand y*, questions remain as to the power of advertising to change people's deeply held beliefs.

Music industry example: The Wave Aid concert held to benefit the Asian tsunami victims successfully built an emotional appeal that raised significant amounts of relief funds.

Briefing an advertising or creative agency

If you plan to engage the services of an external service provider such as an advertising agency, graphic artist or web developer, you will need to provide them with a comprehensive briefing of your promotional requirements. This 'brief' will take the form of a short report called a **copy platform**.

The purpose of the copy platform is to provide the 'creatives' with the essential marketing information that will allow them to build the collateral (marketing materials) you need. It is critical that you develop a sound marketing strategy before approaching any kind of creative agency. Creatives need direction, reference points and boundaries in order to develop collateral. If your strategy is unclear, naturally the results will be mixed. Creative strategy can only be developed from marketing strategy. The undirected creative is an expensive, rudderless ship. Moreover, you do not need creatives dictating marketing strategy when they may not be qualified to do so.

Copy platforms include:
- product/service profiles including USPs (unique selling propositions)
- target audience profiles
- market positioning strategy
- any market research material supporting your strategic direction
- themes, appeals and slogans you may have already developed
- existing and past examples of marketing material.

Media planning

A **media plan** seeks to resolve the following questions:
- Will the selected media mix meet the objectives of the IMC?
- With whom shall we spend our advertising budget?
- Which media types reach our target market?
- What percentage of your target market corresponds to the target audience of the selected media?

- How often shall we place adverts?
- What are the cost-benefits of each media type?

Some definitions

Media mix

This refers to the combination of broadcast, print, outdoor and on-line advertising used to create impact in the minds of the target audience and thus, meet the objectives of the IMC.

Media vehicle

These are the actual programs, publications and websites that advertising is placed in and around. A television media vehicle would *60 Minutes* and a radio example would be *Merrick & Rosso*. A print media vehicle would be *Rolling Stone* and a website media vehicle would be *NineMSN*.

Reach

Reach is the **number of target audience members** exposed to an individual media vehicle and one point in time. Reach is measured on television and radio by the ratings, which is the number of people in each demographic group that are watching or listening to a given media vehicle. The highest rating television programs on Australian free-to-air television often have audiences in excess of two million people. This means that the advertisements attached to that program have significant reach into the homes and minds of Australians.

Frequency

Frequency refers to the number of times a target audience member is exposed to a given media vehicle. Consider a television programme with an audience of two-million. If we were to place an advertisement for a new chill-out album during this program, we would have incredible reach, with a theoretical exposure to over 10% of the Australian population. Yet since we are probably an under-funded record label marketing department, which could probably only afford one advert, a frequency of **one** (advert) is not enough to have significant impact on sales. The message would be too fleeting.

Reach verses frequency

Media planning, no matter the scale, is a balancing act between these two variables. Will enough people see the advert? If they see it once only, will it make a difference? How many times can we afford to run it? Cheaper advertising rates at a smaller publication will mean greater frequency – we can afford more ads, but what about the reach?

Target audience rating point (TARP)

TARPs measure the **reach** of a given media vehicle. Developed by media research agencies on behalf of free-to-air and pay television and radio broadcasters, TARPs are an expression of audience exposure or **ratings**. For example, a television program (media vehicle) might have a TARP of 4 – or, in other words, exposure to 4% of a target audience.

Fleeting

Fleeting messages are those that quickly fade from the memory of those who are exposed to them. Think of the metropolitan daily newspapers. An advertisement in a local daily has a life of one day, while an advertisement in a monthly magazine has a life of 30 days. While the magazine advertisement is less fleeting, this publication probably has a smaller readership and, therefore, less reach than the newspaper.

Media timing and scheduling

How often will you place your advertisements? Will you place them continually, week after week, or will your scheduling be intermittent (or fleeting)? What about a continuous campaign with periodic pulses of increased activity to emphasise special offers or new brands?

Selectivity

Selectivity refers to the varied target audiences available in a particular medium. Compare free-to-air and pay TV in Australia. Pay TV is regarded as having greater selectivity due to the wide variety of channels and program types available to advertisers. By contrast, free-to-air television is more generalist as it caters for the majority of the television audience. Yet on free-to-air some selectivity is possible. For example, Network Ten sees its target audience as the young, while Networks Seven and Nine compete for families and older generations.

Clutter

Clutter refers to the volume of advertising competing for a reader's, listener's or watcher's attention. Music street publications are often guilty of creating too much clutter. Open you local street press and you will notice page after page of black and white ads filled to the brim with text and images. Once in while you will see an advertisement that dares to leave some blank space – these are the advertisements stand out. They demand our attention because they break the pattern of clutter.

Cost per 1000 exposures

This is a measure of the cost of reaching the target audience in units of 1000 people. The basic formula for measuring newspaper and magazine advertising is as follows:

$$\text{CPM (cost per 1000)} \quad = \quad \frac{\text{Cost of ad space}}{\text{Circulation}} \times 1000$$

CASE STUDY - Media Buying

Imagine you a developing an integrated marketing communications plan for an artist that is targeting pre-teen and teenage girls. You would like to place some some advertisements in the monthly glossy magazines targeting these markets. Your plan is to place a full-colour advertisement on the back cover of one magazine that targets the pre-teens and one that targets the teens. You gather the following information to aid your decision.

Title	Magazine profile	Core target audience	Audited	Cost of one full-colour back cover	CPM (per 1000)
Total Girl	*Total Girl* is funky, bright, busy and changes regularly to keep girls stimulated. *Total Girl* exists as an aspirational friend with all the news, trends, gossip and fads for the girl-tween market. A bible of fashion, beauty, fun and everything a girl needs to know. [1]	6-12 year old girls	92,316 [1]	$4610 [1]	$49.93
Smash Hits	The *Smash Hits* reader is typically an excitable female teen between 12 and 17 years of age. They know what the latest superstar trends are and model themselves on their favourite pop singer. [2]	12-17 year old girls	47084 [2]	$4500 [2]	$95.57
Barbie	*Barbie* magazine readers are hip, cool and active girls who love to have heaps of fun. Our readers love to collect *Barbie* magazine and read every part of it from front to back. Mums have a read too! It's true! [2]	6-12 year old girls	68,282 [2]	$3850 [2]	$56.38
Girlfriend	*Girlfriend* is the first stop for 12-19 year-old girls wanting to explore life, have fun, learn, grow and challenge their inner boundaries. [1]	12-19 year old girls	131,348 [1]	$12,350 [1]	$94.02
Dolly	*Dolly* covers every aspect of a girl's life from fashion, health and beauty to celebrities, entertainment and social issues. *Dolly* provides readers with a guide to life and the content is relevant to what is hot and happening each month. *Dolly*... relates to teenagers on their own level – it's a valued friend and confidante.[3]	14-17 year old girls	165,264 [3]	$16,380 [3]	$99.11

1 Pacific Magazines (online), **www.pacificpubs.com.au**
2 Emap Australia (online), **www.emap.com.au**
3 ACP Magazines (online), **www.acp.com.au/magazinetitles**

Case Study continued...

*Note: Advertising agencies can calculate CPM (per 1000) on either **circulation** or on **readership**. Barbie magazine, for example, has audited circulation of 47,084 and an actual readership of 234,000. This means that where audited readership figures are available, the CPM per 1000 works out to be lower. In the Barbie case: \$4500/234,000 = \$19.23 (CPM per 1000). Lower, however, does not mean cheaper. For the Barbie ad you are still paying \$4500, only your reach is greater. Be sure when reviewing the CPM of various publications that you use only one yardstick to compare.

Questions

1 Which magazines would you select and why?
2 What trade-offs might you make between reach and frequency?
3 What other criteria would you use to compare the publications?

Evaluating music media advertising

Media type	Disadvantages	Vehicle examples
Free-to-air television	Limited selectivity Fleeting messages High airtime cost High production cost Clutter	Rove Live The Simpsons
Pay television	Lower market coverage than free-to-air Fleeting messages High airtime cost High production cost Clutter	Channel V MTV History Channel Fox Sports Movie Channel
Commercial	Limited to audio only Fleeting messages Ads often annoying as they need to cut through the clutter	Triple M 2 Day FM Mix 106 Nova FM
Music street press	Short shelf life Clutter, therefore competition for the reader's attention Poor print reproduction and paper quality	Beat Magazine The Brag Drum Media OTS
Glossy music magazines	Longer lead times for artwork production and ad placement Visual only	Blunt Rolling Stone Smash Hits Urban Hitz
Outdoor	Short exposure time Simple messages only Poor image Visual pollution Local planning restrictions	Billboards, buses and bus shelters, taxis, street signage, sky writing and airships

Marketing Plan Builder

Use the Marketing Plan Builder template to develop your music marketing plan. At the conclusion of each chapter the Builder will add a new section to assist in the planning process.

Stage seven: Developing a creative strategy & media plan

With our communication objectives in place, it is now time to decide on the appropriate mix of messages and media by which to tell your story.

1   Create a copy platform (described earlier) to brief any external media, creative or advertising agency who might develop your promotional or campaign material.

_____

_____

_____

2   What type of appeal (emotional, rational, moral) will feature in your campaign materials?

_____

_____

_____

3   Develop a list of the most appropriate broadcast, print and outdoor advertising media that you believe appropriate to your target audience.

_____

_____

_____

4   Contact the individual media outlets and request rate cards (prices) and readership/audience profiles.

_____

_____

_____

marketing plan builder

5   Ask for TARP ratings for individual broadcast media vehicles.

_____

_____

6   Request readership and audited circulation figures of print media vehicles.

_____

_____

7   Begin to brainstorm creative ideas. Try to think of a unique selling proposition, in other words, a killer idea. Tag lines and slogans may need to be developed – remember all such ideas must originate from the product positioning strategy, the target audience profile and the brand theme and message.

_____

_____

_____

_____

_____

thebiz – music business portal

www.thebiz.com.au
Download digital version of the
Marketing Plan Builder

Study questions

1   What is the purpose of a copy platform? Who will read it and what information should it include?

2   Campaign appeals are critical to integrated marketing communications plans. What are the main types of appeals? Which are most suitable for marketing music product?

3   What is a media mix?

4   Evaluate the various forms of advertising used by music marketers. Which have the greatest impact and why?

5   Explain the concept of reach verses frequency in media planning?

6   List some examples of both broadcast and print media vehicles that are effective in reaching music consumers.

7   Clutter and fleeting message impact are significant challenges for media planners. What are they, and how can they be circumvented?

8   Today's audiences are said to be fragmented, due to an increasing variety of media. Why is this of importance to media planners?

Chapter Eight

ONLINE MARKETING, DIRECT MARKETING & SALES PROMOTION

Learning outcomes

By the end of this chapter you should be able to:
- develop online marketing strategies
- evaluate website offerings
- evaluate the role of direct marketing music products
- define the role of sales promotion in music marketing.

Online music marketing

Like all elements of an integrated marketing communications plan, online marketing plays a crucial role. Clearly, the internet is revolutionising music marketing by allowing individual artists to create global music distribution opportunities that were unthinkable a decade ago. This section deals mostly with tactical approaches to online music promotion, since online distribution has been covered in earlier chapters.

While many people believe the internet has rewritten the rules of marketing; that somehow the new medium does not conform to traditional marketing theory and practice. The truth is that the fundamental premise marketing management - market/customer orientation has not changed, only we now have an additional medium by which to communicate with the market.

Setting objectives for online marketing

Like all components of the IMC, websites must be developed in the context of a clear set of objectives. Here is a list of objectives to consider:

- To build brand awareness
- To data mine – or to develop a subscriber database
- To conduct market research
- To generate sales leads
- To streamline distribution systems
- To develop and maintain customer relationships
- To provide real-time information for supply chain participants

Developing an artist website

Your site **look and feel** must be relative to your marketing and integrated communications strategy. The term web design is a deceptive one. While many creative people might believe they can design a website, this is only half the story. Successfully implemented websites incorporate product databases, e-commerce engines, message boards and other 'back-end' or server applications. These structures are created by web developers (and not necessarily web designers) Working in tandem designers and developers create blend the creative with the functional – the colour with the code. Lurking beneath the surface of many-a-funky website is a complex computer code.

Do not underestimate the benefits of engaging outside help. Given the availability of web design software you may be tempted to go DIY. However, if you plan to make money (either directly or indirectly) from your site then it is critical that you engage a professional.

Once you have found your web designer, include the following information in your **design brief**:

- Never forget needs and aspirations of your market or audience.
- Set objectives for the website.
- Emulate successful band websites. Since music itself is a derivative art form, why not web design.
- Ensure that the site has a sense of continuity. A consistent look and feel is critical
- K.I.S.S. – keep it simple stupid. In your rush to create an amazing site – consider how practical and easy to use your site will be.
- Try to make any information no more than '3 clicks away'.
- Make your site is quick to load and easy to navigate.
- Ensure that site content is easy to update. This is particularly important for pages that display the dates/time/venues of your live performances.
- Use colour, fonts and images in a coordinated fashion.
- Make your site search engine friendly. Many interactive sites (such as those using Flash animation) can provide engaging user experiences, yet are problematic for many search engines to scope out. Search engines typically sift through the code on websites looking for key words and links that might propel your site to the top of a search list. The lesson; create a funky interactive site, but do not neglect the main game in e-marketing – search engine optimisation. (SOE)

Emailing a fan database

Directly marketing to fans via email is an essential tool for not only independent artists but also for major record companies. It is relatively easy to gather the email address of fans and use the resulting contact list to provide fans with product updates, live shows details, street crew activities and more. Both the interactive and personalised nature of email marketing can deliver great benefits to the artist.

Email notices can be sent as simple text messages or in more creative ways. The email flyer of solo artist Matt Ellis (see Artist Profile on the following page) has a number of features:

- It's integrated with the entire communications strategy.
- It's useful branding/awareness tool.
- It displays gig information.
- The entire flyer links to the homepage of Matt's site.
- It contains 'hotlinks' to the e-commerce section of his website where people can purchase CDs.
- It contains links to both the record company and the independent distribution company responsible for the album releases.
- Sponsorship cross-promotion – Matt's flyer also contains a hotlink to a leading Australian guitar builder with whom he has sponsorship arrangements.

ARTIST PROFILE – Matt Ellis

A lesson integrated marketing communication

Excerpts from Matt Ellis's bio

Once the front man and founder of hard rockers
Sedgwick Pie, who supported Reef from UK,
Grinspoon and Tumbleweed, Matt Ellis has
now been a thriving solo artist for five years. He
launched his most anticipated self-titled second
album, late 2004.

Matt Ellis - Email flyer

Since releasing the debut album *Peel* in late 2000, Matt Ellis has rarely come up for air.
While the reviewers raved, the audiences packed in and unashamedly screamed for more
at his every show. 'An intriguing debut from a striking talent' wrote Michael Smith, Editor of
The Drum Media. *Revolver*'s Simon Tracy bluntly stated 'The songs? Structured but raw and
diverse. The playing? Fucking fantastic.' Other reviews from *Juice*, *Rolling Stone* and *The
Ozmusic Project* affirmed that *Peel* was 'an independent release of the highest quality by a
brilliant, emerging Australian artist'.

Matt Ellis - CD cover

Matt Ellis the album, is drenched in the moody and atmospheric pop
sensibilities that Matt Ellis the singer/songwriter is renowned for.
Jon Howell's solid beats, Sean Windsor's haunting violins, Johnny
Gauci's Hammond soundscapes and Michael Rix's down-to-earth
bass lines highlight Matt's powerful voice, acoustic guitars and
enigmatic lyrics. Be driven by the energy of 'On Your Way', infected
by the melodies of 'All You Need' and surrender to the sweet gloom
of 'Like It Here'. The previous singles appear too, this time mixed
by Jorden Brebach, who mixed all 12 tracks enhancing its natural,
rootsy production.

2005 is already shaping up to be another frantic year for this restless talent.
www.mattellis.org version 2 has already been launched and will soon host 'On Your Way',
the first music video from the new album scheduled to be launched in February. The release
of this video will be supported by more touring here in Australia and overseas. With a spot on
the Cockatoo Island Festival at Easter and plans to spend extended periods of time playing in
both North America and Europe this year, 2005 could well be the year the world discovers Matt
Ellis. (**www.mattellis.org/biography.php**)

Matt and his management team have created a cleverly designed and integrated promotional
tool. He uses elegant design that is integrated throughout his entire promotional campaign.
Web, print, email flyers and the cover of his latest self-titled release conform to the striking art
direction that flows across all elements of
his promotional mix.

Study questions

1   Evaluate Matt's visual identity. What
    lessons can we learn from the art
    direction?
2   Read over the biography excerpt. What
    do notice about the writing style? Does
    it effectively paint a verbal picture of the
    artist?
3   Visit Matt's website and assess its
    useability. Base your assessment on
    the guidelines for effective website
    design featured earlier in this chapter.

Matt Ellis Website

Direct marketing

Direct marketing is a mode of marketing used by organisations to create and maintain personal relationships with individual customers. This is largely achieved through interactive technologies that allow firms to bypass traditional supply chains and market directly to customers in any location in the world. The interactive technologies used by direct marketers are:

- **Customer / fan databases** – allowing music marketers to target individual customers with unique product/service offerings. (See marketing highlight on the following page).
- **Email marketing** – once a database is established then individual customers can be sent flyers, updates and promotional offers. (See Matt Ellis email flyer.)
- **SMS / text marketing** – the mobile phone numbers of your database members can be sent promotional material in the form of text, audio, pictures and movies.
- **Internet** – websites, when integrated with a competition give-away, can yield valuable additions to your customer database. This process is called **data mining** and involves the collection of customer contact information.
- **Telemarketing** – despite the negative view that many consumers have of tele-salespeople calling your home or business, the practice is in fact an critical element of business-to-business marketing in particular.
- **Direct mail** – involves the postage of printed marketing materials directly to consumers. Direct marketing ranges from unsolicited, random junk mail offers through to mail campaigns where prospective customers have given their permission to be mailed.

Marketing highlight – Artist home invasion

Australian artists Deborah Conway and Willy Zygier have created an innovative method of direct marketing their music. Coinciding with the release of their 2004 album, *Summertown*, this acoustic pop act created the novel concept of **Summerware parties**. A neat parallel to the Tupperware party, Conway & Zygier arrange to play in-home gigs at the request of fans. In order to hold a party, fans must guarantee a certain (yet modest) number of people to attend who will buy the CD. If ever there was evidence music distribution is undergoing a cottage industry direct marketing revolution this is it.

Marketing highlight – Customer relationship management (CRM)

As the name indicates, the goal of CRM is to create and maintain profitable relationships with customers. Historically, CRM, say for a small business was a relatively simple affair. Think of a suburban corner store. The owner probably knows most customers by name, is aware of their individual likes, dislikes, regular purchases and even family their gossip! Consider then, larger businesses who are trying to re-create the kind of relationship you have with your local grocer, only they use information technology in their attempt to form strong (profitable) bonds with you.

At the core of CRM therefore, are relationships. If we assume that a firm has a relationship with a customer, would that customer regard the firm as a friend? Well the Oxford dictionary defines a friend as; "one joined to another in mutual benevolence and intimacy".[1] In addition Michael Argyle and Monica Henderson at Oxford University defined several basic universal rules of friendship. Among them: provide emotional support, respect privacy, and preserve confidences, and be tolerant of other friendships.[2]

CRM uses of database technology designed of course to sell more products and services through the development of supposedly, mutually beneficial relationships. Yet firms must be tolerant of a your friendship with other brands. Relationships must be based on mutual benevolence, and firms must respect your privacy and provide emotional support. Well, we are sure you have probably not experienced this kind of relationship from all the companies that claim to be in a relationship with you.

Situations where CRM technology is used in the entertainment industry include:

* Interactive direct marketing - this involves instant messaging and email campaigns targeting the mobile phone numbers and email addresses collected from fans who have bought tickets for an outdoor event.

* The use of email lists by record companies to micro-target fans of a niche market album release that does not have significant radio airplay. This can work well if the CD cannot find wide enough retail distribution, yet enough fans will buy the CD directly from the label for it to be profitable.

* Unsigned artists gathering and maintaining a list of fan email addresses through which to promote gigs, media appearances, single and album releases and airplay requests.

* Street-crew management – as a street crew grows in size there is no other option than to compile a computer database of their contact details, activities and rewards.

* Using a band website to run competitions in order to gather email addresses that can be used to direct market.

Study questions

1   Describe ways in which you could create CRM opportunities in your music business.
2   Does traditional media advertising have a future given the increasing importance of CRM and the direct marketing of entertainment?
3   How will CRM and the direct marketing recorded music impact on retail CD sales?

Assessing direct marketing

Advantages	Disadvantages
Tailored messages.	Direct mail cost per customer contact is high.
Deeper customer relationships.	List quality can be variable.
Highly segmented lists are available.	May be perceived as spam or junk mail.
High frequency – particularly with low cost media like email.	High frequency may mean highly annoyed prospective customers.
Bypasses mass media, which has higher absolute costs.	Anti-spam laws create compliance challenges.
Email marketing cost per customer contact is low.	Telemarketing has a poor image.
Call centres from developing nations reduce costs of telemarketing.	Response rates (or the number of people responding) are low, particularly for junk style direct mail.
Consumers are increasing their dependence on SMS and email.	
Development of more powerful database technology.	
Direct marketing is an effective link between promotional mix elements.	
Increasing evidence that permission-based direct marketing campaigns (where the mailing list is comprised of people who have volunteered their contact details) have higher than average response rates.	

Sales promotion and music

Sales promotion tactics are used to provide incentive for customers to purchase. They encourage, compel and even cajole shoppers into making immediate purchase decisions.

Since most markets (including that of music) are bursting with competing, similar products, providing customers with incentives to purchase (via sales promotion) has become increasingly important. Sales promotion can be categorised in two ways: those promotions that target consumers and those that target the participants in the distribution channel.

Consumer oriented sales promotion targets the end users of products in an attempt to stimulate demand. Also known as a 'pull' strategy, since rising consumer demand for a product forces distributors and retailers to stock the products, effectively pulling the products through the distribution channel.

Trade oriented sales promotion targets the distribution and retail channel partners. It encourages the channel to stock and then actively promote the products either to retail customers, or to other members of the channel. Known as a 'push' strategy, since it attempts to force the channel to give customers access to products.

Push and pull sales promotion - see page 75 for a model of sales promotion in the record industry

Comparing consumer and trade oriented sales promotion

Promotion type	Consumer sales promotion (demand pull)	Trade sales promotion (demand push)
Competitions and prize draws	Offers directly to fans and street-crews	Incentive promotions to CD retailers, their management and staff
Street promotion and street-crew activities	yes	no
Promotional CDs	no	yes
Bonus tracks on CDs	no	yes
In-store promotion with CD retailers In-store point-of-sale promotional material Artist appearances, signings and performances Posters and print collateral Listening posts End-of-aisle product displays	yes	yes
Radio promotion	yes	no
Live performance to public	yes	no
Live performance – industry showcases	no	yes

Competitions and prize-draws

Competitions are not only useful in promoting immediate sales or eliciting response from customers, they are also an important data-mining tool. This means that when you run a competition and ask people to 'enter their details online and go into the draw to win stuff', you are collecting or 'mining' their contact details, which you will later use in your direct marketing activities.

Under state and territory laws in Australia, competitions may have to be registered with the appropriate state department of gaming and racing. It is advised that you contact the gaming and racing authorities in your state for the relevant rules and guidelines.

thebiz – music business portal

www.thebiz.com.au
Find links to these government departments.

Street crew promotion

In recent times sales promotion via street crew marketing has emerged as an important weapon in the arsenal of the music manager. Pioneered in the mid-1990s by bands such as Linkin Park recruited fans across the world to join their official 'street crew'. Using the Internet as the unifying force, Linkin Park was able to extend the passive role of the fan club into an active component of the band's marketing machine.

Examples of street crew deployment include:

- **Seeding chat rooms** – where street crew members 'talk-up' the band in the message boards of websites relevant to existing and potential fans. Linkin Park initially targeted fan message boards of bands like Limp Bizkit, and spread the word amongst these like-minded individuals.

- **Message board champions** – better than simply employing people to artificially talk-up the band, is to identify chat-roomers who are already champions for the cause. In this case, the band or management participate in a message board forum, identify hard core fans of the band and then approach them to become street crew members. This way their future chat room promotional efforts would be more powerful than a paid, perhaps disinterested, person.

- **E-teaming** – creating and distributing electronic flyers, cards, animations, web-links and email promotions to friends and contacts. This typically involves building profiles via the major online communities such as MySpace.

- **Chalking** – using chalk to graffiti promotional messages on the street pavements. Commonly web addresses are chalked on street corners.

- **Promotional flyers (handbills)** – street crew can be deployed handing out flyers, CD samplers and merchandise on street corners and other public places. Depending on the way they are used, street crew can be more cost effective than paying a sales promotion firm to do the same job.

- **CD store listening posts** – street crew can be used to listen to your CDs in-store and engage other customers directly or indirectly, promoting the band.

- **Ambient conversation** – street crew members simply chat about the coolest band (ie *your* band) whenever they are on public transport, in a café, at school or any other public place where the target audience hangs out. Next time you hear a couple of teenagers loudly discussing music on the train, perhaps they want you to listen!

What better way to spread the word than through committed fans? The rewards for street crew are:
- peer status – the prestige of being an official member of the street crew
- assisting in the success of your favourite band/artist
- free and discounted merchandise
- advance access to new albums and singles
- *street crew members only* sections on official band websites
- invitations to band dress rehearsals
- competitions and prize give-aways
- priority seating/ticketing for concerts
- autographed photos and merchandise
- attending meet and greet sessions with the band/artist

Marketing highlight – Experiential marketing

(Stunt, guerilla, viral and ambient marketing)

The recent explosion in both the volume and variety of media directed at consumers has resulted in a marked decline in the effectiveness of many approaches to promotion. There is simply too much media cluttering up people's lives and message impact is declining.

This abundance of advertising media and the encouraged further fragmentation of consumers into more highly defined (and refined) target audiences means that it can be tricky to orchestrate a marketing campaign. How do you create campaigns that have the reach, frequency and punch to affect change in the minds of consumers?

Marketers have for many decades recognised the value of word-of-mouth communication, where consumers spread good reports about products and services they enjoy. The challenge has always been to develop tactical promotional tools designed to create positive word-of-mouth – this is where the experiential marketing comes into play. Experiential marketing, or marketing (and/or promotion) that you experience or participate in, includes a variety of techniques.

Marketing highlight cont.

Technique	Description	Suggested tactic
Ambient marketing	A form of experiential marketing that attempts to surround the lives of consumers. Like ambient music, it is designed to create an atmosphere that weaves in and out of your everyday life. It is less confrontational than traditional forms of advertising.	Approach a fresh produce distribution company and pay to have small band sticker on every apple and orange sold via fruit stalls.
Viral marketing	Like a biological virus, this form of marketing is supposed to self-replicate. Viral techniques rely on customers and employees to perpetuate advertising messages to friends, family and colleagues. Its effectiveness lies in exploiting the trusted relationships people have with each other. Messages are mostly disseminated via powerful word-of-mouth communication.	Deploy street crew to listening posts at CD retailers and anonymously encourage store customers to 'sample' the compilation. Enlist hairdressers and beauty therapists to spread the word to their customers, who may be your customers. Give them free CDs, merchandise and concert tickets and encourage them to play your music.
Stunt marketing	An extension of the old-fashioned publicity stunt. It seems that as long as you attach the word 'marketing' to the end of a sales promotion tactic then you have a new form of marketing.	If you are a controversial band, deploy your street crew to protest your own gig. Seek media coverage, and heighten your mojo status as teenagers are inspired by rebellion.
Guerilla marketing	Targeted at competitors rather than customers. It is built on the premise that business is warfare and that it is probably smarter not to attack enemies head on. Rather use stealthy guerrilla tactics to defeat competition. The key is also to spend little to gain a lot.	Distribute promotional flyers to punters entering and leaving a competitor's premises.

marketing plan builder

Marketing Plan Builder

Use the Marketing Plan Builder template to develop your music marketing plan. At the conclusion of each chapter the Builder will add a new section to assist in the planning process.

Stage eight: Developing online marketing, direct marketing and sales promotion

Consider the following tasks in planning online and direct marketing and sales promotion:

1. Do you need a website? If so, spend some time evaluating the websites of successful artists in your genre.

2. List the features and resources you wish to make available to your potential website visitors.

3. Develop ways of drawing traffic to your website by integrating the site address (URL) into off-line promotions.

4. Develop a means of mining the data of site visitors. Online competition registrations, street crew membership and message boards are ways of making your site interactive, rather than just an online brochure – and you can add their contact and demographic information to your database.

5. Learn to use customer relationship management (CRM) software. Plug in your database of contacts and begin to direct market to your list.

6. Begin to develop sales promotion ideas. List the types of competitions, price discounts and other sales promotion elements you can either push to the distribution channel or to stimulate demand at the consumer end.

⊙ ⊙ ⊙   thebiz – music business portal

www.thebiz.com.au
Download digital version of the
Marketing Plan Builder

Study questions

1   Describe some useful objectives for a band website.

2   What are the differences between a website designer and a website developer?

3   Many bands are now simply using their MySpace page as their website. Is MySpace a valid alternative to the traditional band website? Justify your argument.

4   What is direct marketing?

5   Direct marketing has become a significant component of every promotional campaign. What social, cultural technological changes have led to this?

6   Describe some benefits of direct email campaigns for music product?

7   What are the differences between trade and consumer oriented sales promotion?

8   Are street crews appropriate for all artists? What genres of artist might benefit most from a street crew strategy?

9   What are the two possible types of competitions and prize draws available for music marketers?

10 List some experiential marketing techniques. Do you believe these 'new' forms of promotion are just fads, or will they become major components of all future integrated communication strategies?

Chapter Nine

PUBLIC RELATIONS, PUBLICITY & IMAGE DEVELOPMENT

Learning outcomes

By the end of this chapter you should be able to:

- evaluate the role of publicity in music marketing
- evaluate the role of public relations in music marketing
- develop publicity materials

What are public relations?

The Australian Public Relations Institute (APRIA) defines public relations (PR) as:

> 'Deliberate, planned and sustained effort to establish and maintain mutual understanding between an organisation and its publics'.

Managing an artist's public relations is the management of relationships with **publics**. Basically, PR is doing good things and telling others about it.

What therefore is a 'public', and why is it so important to manage one? The term public refers to any identifiable group, organisation, individual or group of individuals with whom the band has an ongoing relationship. The music media (newspapers, radio etc), for example, is a key public with whom the artist will have a relationship. Clearly the effective management of relationships with key music journalists will have significant impact on the artist success.

An artist and the external publics

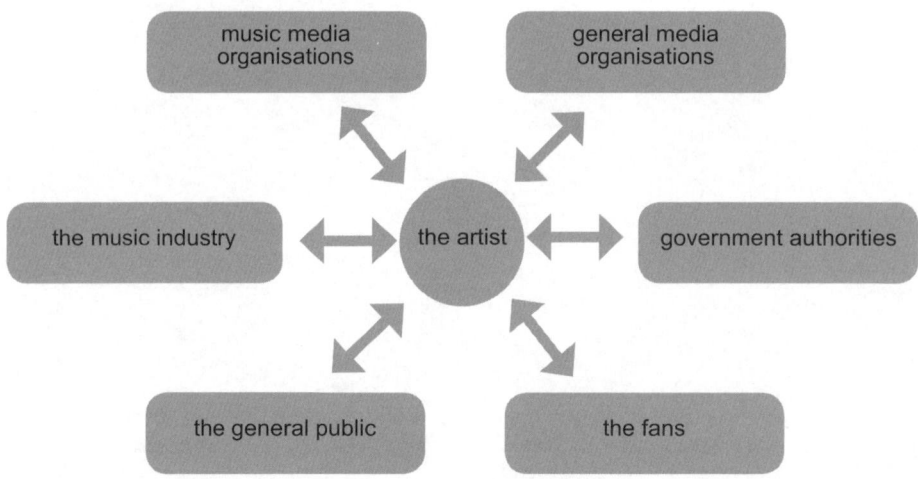

What is publicity?

Publicity is the end result of public relations. If you relate well to the music press, then this *public* may provide you the editorial coverage required to build fame. The benefits of publicity through editorial are:

- **It's free** – Journalists write stories about the events, people or products they believe the reading/listening public will find it interesting or newsworthy. Are you worthy of being regarded as news? Will your target audience stop to read a story about you?
- **It's unbiased** – In a perfect world journalists would be free of influence and would relate unbiased balanced views on newsworthy events. We do not, of course, live in a perfect world, so journalists can be swayed. It is your job to sway them, ethically. If this means you need to give them free tickets to you gig then so be it.

The media release

The media (or press) release is the standard means of communicating newsworthy information to journalists. In written form, the media release commonly consists of 300-500 words over one to two pages.

Why send a media release?

Journalists and editors expect to be informed in the standard media release format. The media release serves the following functions:

- Allows the sender greater control over the facts contained in the story. This simply means that if you a publicising a CD launch you can send the crucial event details (date, time and location) set in a clear, non-confusing manner.
- Editorial staff (journalists) then do not have to verify the essential information. It is all there in black and white.
- Media releases either by fax, mail or email allow you to send to many journalists/publications simultaneously.
- Publications will often print your 'story' word-for-word.
- Editorial coverage is low or no cost.
- Editorial comment is viewed by readers as being less biased than say an advertisement for the same product/event/story.
- In today's hyper-competitive media industry, advertising managers are desperate for your paid advertisements. If you book advertising with a particular publication the advertising sales manager might pass your media release directly to the editorial department and ask them to make space for your 'story'. Clearly this raises some ethical issues regarding a free-press, however, the fact is, money talks. Advertise, and your press release will most probably magically find itself on top of the heap.

Disadvantages of media releases

- Since you haven't paid for the editorial coverage, you have limited control over placement or timing of your media release.
- You also do not control the journalist in question, who may in fact choose to write a negative story about your product or event – or simply ignore it!
- The journalist may cover your story and incorrectly represent the 'facts' you supplied them.

Will they print it?

Despite our ability as marketers to leverage paid advertising space against editorial coverage, the publication is unlikely to run the story if it is not newsworthy. It must be of significant interest to the readership otherwise the publication will diminish its standing amongst readers. This is true for most publications and media outlets that place high value on their journalist integrity. However there are many publications that are more than happy to compromise for the sake of advertising revenue.

What newsworthy things can a band do?

- Single, album and EP release and launch parties
- New band members
- New recording, publishing and distribution deals
- Commence recording new material
- Charity events and social causes the band is involved with
- Becoming the support for a major touring act
- Being included on the bill of a major outdoor music festival
- Band members co-writing with other famous or respected songwriters
- Band members appearing as interviewees on radio and television
- Sales successes – milestones like 5000, 10,000 or more CDs sold
- Chart success – either independent or mainstream chart success is a great source of news for emerging bands.
- Controversial opinions or attitudes of the band members.

Media release layout - Example A

IDENTIFY THE
DOCUMENT

IDENTIFY
THE ORIGIN

NEWSWORTHY
HEADLINE

POWERFUL
OPENING
PARAGRAPH

TIMING OF
RELEASE

DATE

QUOTE A
REVIEWER

ACKNOWLEDGE
A SPONSOR

CONTACT DETAILS

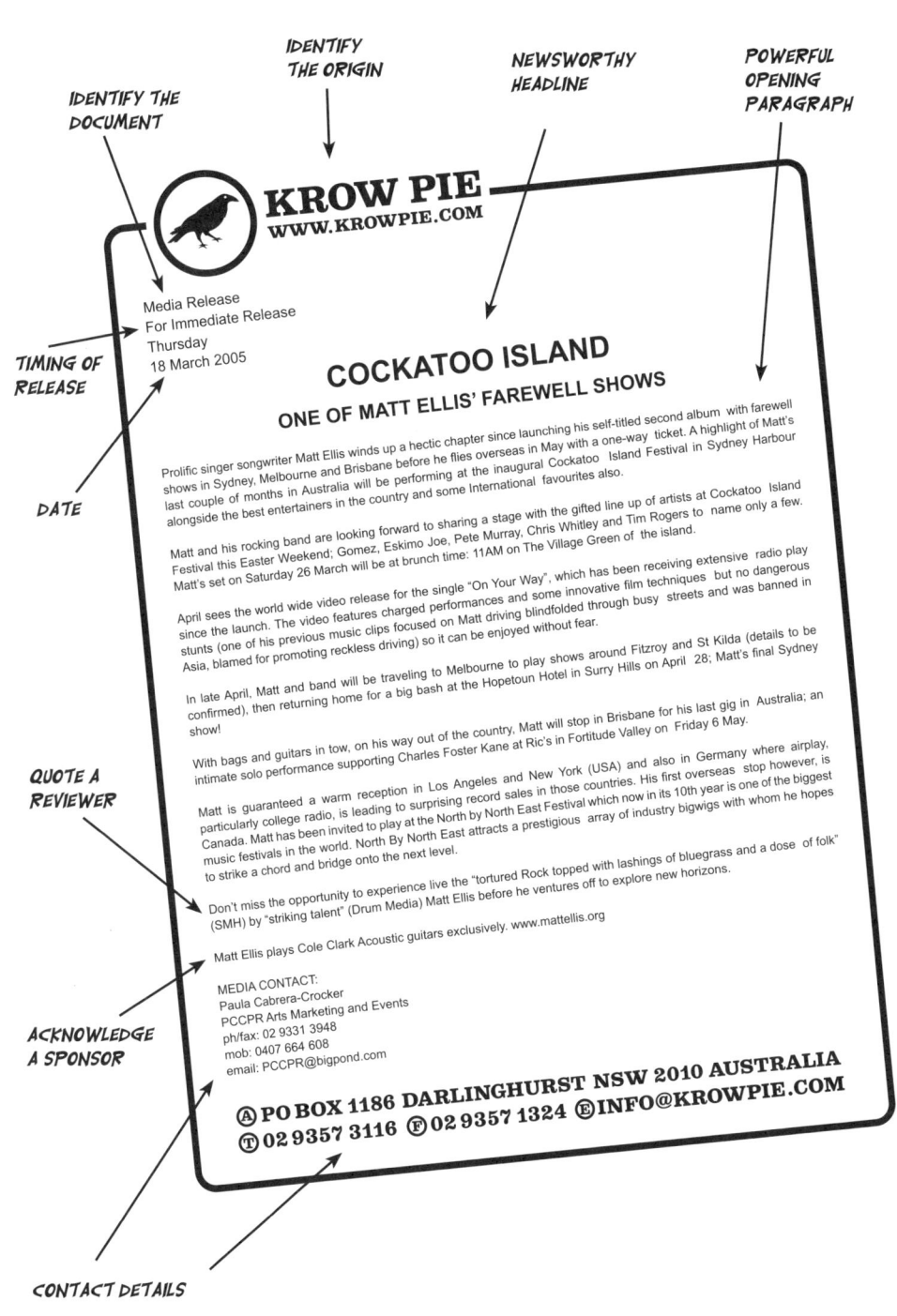

KROW PIE
WWW.KROWPIE.COM

Media Release
For Immediate Release
Thursday
18 March 2005

COCKATOO ISLAND
ONE OF MATT ELLIS' FAREWELL SHOWS

Prolific singer songwriter Matt Ellis winds up a hectic chapter since launching his self-titled second album with farewell shows in Sydney, Melbourne and Brisbane before he flies overseas in May with a one-way ticket. A highlight of Matt's last couple of months in Australia will be performing at the inaugural Cockatoo Island Festival in Sydney Harbour alongside the best entertainers in the country and some International favourites also.

Matt and his rocking band are looking forward to sharing a stage with the gifted line up of artists at Cockatoo Island Festival this Easter Weekend; Gomez, Eskimo Joe, Pete Murray, Chris Whitley and Tim Rogers to name only a few. Matt's set on Saturday 26 March will be at brunch time: 11AM on The Village Green of the island.

April sees the world wide video release for the single "On Your Way", which has been receiving extensive radio play since the launch. The video features charged performances and some innovative film techniques but no dangerous stunts (one of his previous music clips focused on Matt driving blindfolded through busy streets and was banned in Asia, blamed for promoting reckless driving) so it can be enjoyed without fear.

In late April, Matt and band will be traveling to Melbourne to play shows around Fitzroy and St Kilda (details to be confirmed), then returning home for a big bash at the Hopetoun Hotel in Surry Hills on April 28; Matt's final Sydney show!

With bags and guitars in tow, on his way out of the country, Matt will stop in Brisbane for his last gig in Australia; an intimate solo performance supporting Charles Foster Kane at Ric's in Fortitude Valley on Friday 6 May.

Matt is guaranteed a warm reception in Los Angeles and New York (USA) and also in Germany where airplay, particularly college radio, is leading to surprising record sales in those countries. His first overseas stop however, is Canada. Matt has been invited to play at the North by North East Festival which now in its 10th year is one of the biggest music festivals in the world. North By North East attracts a prestigious array of industry bigwigs with whom he hopes to strike a chord and bridge onto the next level.

Don't miss the opportunity to experience live the "tortured Rock topped with lashings of bluegrass and a dose of folk" (SMH) by "striking talent" (Drum Media) Matt Ellis before he ventures off to explore new horizons.

Matt Ellis plays Cole Clark Acoustic guitars exclusively. www.mattellis.org

MEDIA CONTACT:
Paula Cabrera-Crocker
PCCPR Arts Marketing and Events
ph/fax: 02 9331 3948
mob: 0407 664 608
email: PCCPR@bigpond.com

Ⓐ PO BOX 1186 DARLINGHURST NSW 2010 AUSTRALIA
Ⓣ 02 9357 3116 Ⓕ 02 9357 1324 Ⓔ INFO@KROWPIE.COM

Media release layout example B

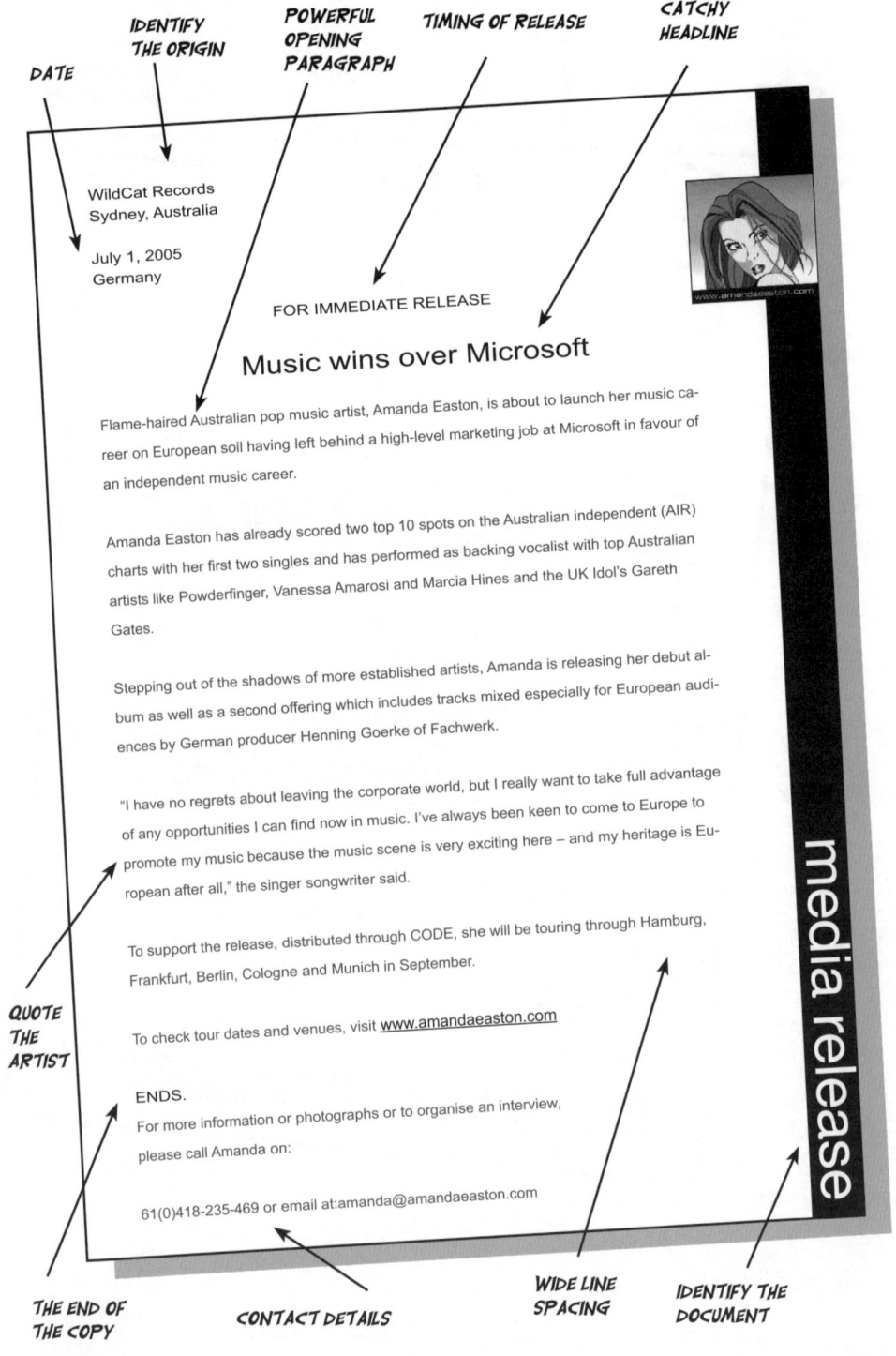

DATE

IDENTIFY THE ORIGIN

POWERFUL OPENING PARAGRAPH

TIMING OF RELEASE

CATCHY HEADLINE

WildCat Records
Sydney, Australia

July 1, 2005
Germany

FOR IMMEDIATE RELEASE

Music wins over Microsoft

Flame-haired Australian pop music artist, Amanda Easton, is about to launch her music career on European soil having left behind a high-level marketing job at Microsoft in favour of an independent music career.

Amanda Easton has already scored two top 10 spots on the Australian independent (AIR) charts with her first two singles and has performed as backing vocalist with top Australian artists like Powderfinger, Vanessa Amarosi and Marcia Hines and the UK Idol's Gareth Gates.

Stepping out of the shadows of more established artists, Amanda is releasing her debut album as well as a second offering which includes tracks mixed especially for European audiences by German producer Henning Goerke of Fachwerk.

"I have no regrets about leaving the corporate world, but I really want to take full advantage of any opportunities I can find now in music. I've always been keen to come to Europe to promote my music because the music scene is very exciting here – and my heritage is European after all," the singer songwriter said.

To support the release, distributed through CODE, she will be touring through Hamburg, Frankfurt, Berlin, Cologne and Munich in September.

To check tour dates and venues, visit www.amandaeaston.com

QUOTE THE ARTIST

ENDS.
For more information or photographs or to organise an interview, please call Amanda on:

61(0)418-235-469 or email at:amanda@amandaeaston.com

media release

THE END OF THE COPY

CONTACT DETAILS

WIDE LINE SPACING

IDENTIFY THE DOCUMENT

Language and style

Consider the following:

- Use a professional copywriter to write or edit your text. Freelance copywriters often charge reasonable hourly rates so it is well worth it for a professional touch.
- Ask a journalist (who's writing style you like) to write your media releases and biographical information.
- Use simple language that is relevant to the readership of the target publications or media outlets.
- Most publications have detailed demographic information on their readership. If you indicate your desire to advertise in a particular publication, the advertising manager or editor will supply you their readership profiles. In fact, many publications make this information freely available in the advertising section of their websites.
- Use concise language – short sentences and short paragraphs. Simple is best.
- If you use descriptive language, be careful not to include too many over-blown adjectives. While vigorous language can lift a story, it cannot make a story newsworthy if it is not.
- Be positive – imagine yourself as the reader. Is the story, and the language it uses, interesting?
- Include quotes – this simple but effective principle allows readers to 'hear it from the horse's mouth'. Readers we are always interested to hear the attitudes and beliefs of band members – it brings them closer to the band.

The opening paragraph

The general rule for media releases is; if the first paragraph is all the reader reads, then make sure all critical information pertaining to the story is contained there. The opening paragraph must attract the readers' attention and hold their interest. Most importantly it must include: who, what, where, when and why. Analyse the opening paragraphs of the media release examples. Do they conform to the five 'W's principle?

Headlines

Headlines give the story impact. They should be eye catching, informative and should have an 'angle'. Headlines might be used by the targeted journalist, who, for the sake of convenience, might simply use the one you have cleverly crafted. Don't assume, however, that journalists will just print whatever you send them. Importantly they have a free will and are not simply your mouthpiece.

Deadlines

Conduct some research on your target publications. When are their publication deadlines? If you're not sure, ring them and ask. This may sound obvious, but some publications have long 'lead' times – for example, a monthly music magazine may have deadlines for certain content at least two weeks in advance of publication. A cleverly integrated communications strategy for your album launch may be compromised because you missed a deadline with a crucial publication.

Embargoes and caveats

An embargo (or caveat) is a restriction the writer of a media release places on its publication date or time. An example where this might be useful is the timing of press coverage relative to other elements of the IMC. You might have advertising, website and SMS promotions carefully timed to integrate with press coverage or a media appearance by the band, and you would like to restrict journalists from releasing the story too early. Generally speaking journalists will honour embargoes, but this cannot be guaranteed. Most often you though, you will place the heading 'For Immediate Release' or 'Release at Will' on the media release.

Press kits and promotional packages

A press kit is the main public and media relations tool used by artists. Traditionally press kits were sent out via the post, this however is changing. Online press kits via the artist website and electronic press kits (EPKs) are increasingly becoming the norm. An EPK is either on video, DVD or sent via an email that includes many of the traditional press kit items. The following table shows the various elements included in the three types of press kits.

Inclusion	Format	Traditional kit	EPK	Media page (artist website)
Band photos	8" x 12" glossy black & white prints	yes	no	no
	JPEG & GIF images	no	yes	yes
	300 dpi (CMYK) TIFF (magazines and newspapers need photos in this high resolution printable format)	no	yes only if CD ROM or DVD	yes
Band bio	Printed	yes	no	no
	Adobe PDF document	no	yes	yes
Media releases	Printed	yes	no	no
	Adobe PDF document	no	yes	yes
Audio samples	CD	yes	no	no
	MP3 or another downloadable audio file format	no	yes	yes
Music video	If sending to a program for TV consult with the producer as to the broadcast video format they require	yes	yes	no
	Video tape & DVD	yes	yes	no
	QuickTime video file	no	yes	yes
Press clippings	Previous editorial coverage from newspapers and magazines	yes	yes	yes

Biographies

Aside from a photo of the band, the biography is the most important component of the press kit. Its role is to provide an overall impression of the band; its formation, personnel, image and style, ambitions and attitudes.

Who reads them?

Industry decision makers who will read your bio include:
- record label executives, such as A&R (artist and repertoire) managers
- record distributors
- music publishers
- record producers
- concert promoters
- venture capitalists (financial backers)
- film and television producers
- record store owners and managers
- music journalists
- prospective artist managers
- booking agents
- event managers
- radio play-list managers and DJs
- fans

What information to include

In order to prepare an effective bio, a band manager must first interview the band. Imagine you are a journalist and you would like to know every detail about the band and its members. Later you can edit the information into a compact format. Here is a list of questions to ask.

1. Where did you meet?
2. When did you form?
3. Who are your favourite bands/artists?
4. What are your musical influences?
5. Which bands do you compare yourselves to?
6. If you saw your CD in a record store, what category would it be under?
7. Describe your typical fan.
8. Where did you grow up?
9. What other bands have you played with?
10. Does the band have formal musical education?
11. What are the ethnic backgrounds of the band members? This should provide some interesting, eclectic information.
12. The back-story to the songs. How were they written? What are they about and how do they relate to your image?
13. Do you do anything unusual while performing live?
14. Do you have any future recording projects or plans?
15. What are your future live or touring plans?
16. What has been your career highlight so far?
17. Any obscure piece of information about the band that might seem irrelevant.

Writing style – Clearly the list of questions above will generate large amounts of information, so careful editing is required. The edited word length of a bio depends on the number of years the band has existed. An act like U2 or AC/DC could have a biography the size of an encyclopedia. For new acts though, a good rule of thumb would be 500 words in length.

Journalists are often suspicious of new bands with long, elaborate bios. The might ask; 'how can they have achieved so much and I have never heard of them?' Alternatively, they simply won't take the time to read a long bio, even those of more established artists. The key therefore is to keep it concise.

The worst biographies are those that are filled with tedious descriptions of band history. While it is important to cover historical issues, avoid comments that resemble: 'Billy quit, Jodie got married ... we then moved house and the drum kit wouldn't fit through the door, so we decided to use a drum machine so we fired Bob (the drummer) ... later that week we did our first gig, Bob turned up and stubbed out his cigarette on the drum machine … then we ... blah, blah …'

Dripping with adjectives? – Be careful not to fill the bio with unsubstantiated tales full of adjectives. Music journalists need the language to be creative without overstating the bands achievements through over-descriptive language. Words that may damage your credibility include 'ground breaking', 'innovative' and 'phenomenal'. Keep it simple and let the journalist draw some conclusions – after all this is his/her job.

Use quotes – Quotations allow readers a glimpse into the mind of the artist. They are a powerful tool in personalising the biography, making it more accessible and not simply the language of a writer.

Format – Generally speaking a biography should be no more than two A4 pages. The purpose of the bio is to quickly and efficiently convey your story to the interested reader, so do not be too clever with page layout and design. While it may seem tempting to load the page with elaborate typesetting, at best this may be distracting, at worst your fancy bio will be passed over in favour of one with a simpler design.

Target your readers – Bios of original artists and those of cover/tribute bands vary significantly. For the tribute band the objective of the bio is to sell the band to a venue or bar manager, who has no interest in history, formation and the philosophy of the band. That person just wants to know that your band will keep punters happy, and spending.

Artist bio example

amandaeaston

www.amandaeaston.com

"these songs are so accessible and melodic you can't quite figure out why she hasn't been snapped up by some major label looking for a real – as against manufactured – pop diva" The Drum Media's (Australia) Michael Smith on Amanda's debut album (out through WildCat Records).

Flame-haired Australian Amanda Easton is a powerful live performer and with her band is often described as the love child of Shirley Manson and Norah Jones. She delivers raunchy jazz-tinged pop-rock music with the passion of an independent but the music is, as Australia's Drum Media says' 'fiercely commercial'. She performed with Powderfinger at the 1999 Australian Music Awards (ARIAs) and has been touring with multi-platinum Australian artist Richard Clapton. She also recently performed with Top 10 artists Vanessa Amarosi and Shakaya as well as Marcia Hines and the UK's Gareth Gates (Pop Idol).

Amanda is in Europe to release her debut album and a second album featuring tracks specifically for the European market. She will tour around the UK, France and Germany performing acoustic gigs with her guitarist. The albums are out through German distributor CODE.

In her home country, Amanda has released two self-penned singles which charted in the top 10 of the Australian independent (AIR) charts and have received airplay on major Australian commercial radio and TV.

"...The power of this track lies with Amanda's impressive vocals which are backed up with a catchy as hell beat and an instantly remembered chorus..pop with substance...offers an edge to anyone fed up with manufactured pop." MUSIC NETWORK MAGAZINE, reviewing Amanda's single 'Celebrity'

"A star-filled night... add the very talented Amanda Easton and you would believe that one of those stars had fallen right on the deck."...Mary Jo, Wentworth Courier.

"Amanda wraps her rich tones around a song...that slinks in the room, and rubs itself up against your leg in a delightfully shiver inducing manner...," Ross Clelland, Drum Media.

Fully self-financed and well-known as one of the hardest working independent artists in Sydney, this darling of the local pop scene is also a dedicated live music promoter, her latest effort being the hugely successful 'PopTarts' showcasing up and coming female pop talent.(www.amandaeaston.com/poptarts)

Amanda spent 16 months singing and songwriting in Japan. She also has two of her self-penned songs on the soundtrack of Australian rock-n-roll road movie 'Second Best bed' planned for production later this year. Amanda is slated to play the lead role. She's also just returned from a tour in Malaysia with her band.

For tour dates and more details please visit www.amandaeaston.com

Contact: Amanda Easton...Mobile: 61(0) 418 235 469...Email: amanda@amandaeaston.com

www.amandaeaston.com

biography

Press kit within a demo CD

This press kit example folds length-ways down to the size of a CD jewel case insert. The arrow indicates how the item is folded. Cleverly, it reduces the need to send separate printed introduction letters, bios and press releases.

KROW PIE
WWW.KROWPIE.COM

RAGE ABC TV
Narelle Gee   Wed 20th March

Hi Narelle,

Please find attached my current bio, a copy of my new self-titled album and the first video to be lifted off it, **On Your Way,** as an application for airplay on RAGE.

The video was shot, edited and directed by my brother Sean Ellis, and brings to life the look and feel of the new album's artwork.

I've recently released my new album and have spent the past few months touring Australia to promote it. In June I'm heading off overseas for an extended period of time to tour, write and record the next album. Thanks again for your time and all your support Narelle. I hope you like the new video!

Yours sincerely,

Matt Ellis.

⊕ PO BOX 1186 DARLINGHURST NSW 2010 AUSTRALIA
⊕ 02 9357 3116 ⊕ 02 9357 1234 ⊕ INFO@KROWPIE.COM

A STRIKING TALENT."

Michael Smith
Drum Media.

**AS UPLIFTING AS IT
IS POWERFUL."**

Zolton Zavos
The Brag.

MEDIA RELEASE

Critically acclaimed singer songwriter Matt Ellis has just launched his self-titled second album to a full house at Sydney's Vanguard Hotel to more rave reviews. Zolton Zarvos from the Brag wrote, "As uplifting as it is powerful", while the SMH described it as "Tortured rock topped with lashings of bluegrass and a dose of folk." The launch performance (like all of Matt's live shows) was so fervently received that he is now taking his distinctive earthy brand of rock pop to new audiences all over Australia and beyond.

Since the launch, Matt has taken his new album on tour to Melbourne, Canberra, Sydney, Newcastle, Byron Bay and Brisbane. Tracks have enjoyed rotation on Triple J, Sydney's FBi Radio, Newcastle's New FM, 2NUR and countless community stations Australia wide. "Matt Ellis" is now available in Europe through Glitter House (www.glitterhouse.com) and has begun to receive airplay on College radio in Germany.

Aware that making it in the music industry can be a profound struggle, Matt has taken control of his musical career by being active in all aspects involved. Some of his achievements to date include a self funded promotional tour of the United States and Asia to support the release of his debut solo album "Peel", appearing live on Channel [V] Asia, receiving radio airplay of all his releases in most continents and averaging 10,000 hits a week on his website... but more importantly, when he plays live, the crowd always screams for more!

"Matt Ellis", the album is drenched in the moody and atmospheric pop sensibilities that Matt Ellis the singer songwriter is renowned for. Jon Howell's solid beats, Sean Windsor's haunting violins, Johnny Gauci's Hammond soundscapes and Michael Rix's down-to-earth bass lines highlight Matt's powerful voice, acoustic guitars and enigmatic lyrics. Be driven by the energy of "On Your Way", infected by the melodies of "All You Need" and surrender to the sweet gloom of "Like It Here". Out now on his Krow Pie label, distributed by MGM and therefore available at all good music stores, it was co-produced by ARIA award winner Jonathan Burnside, Matt Ellis himself and his long time musical collaborator, Tamlin.

Matt Ellis plays Cole Clark Acoustic guitars exclusively.

Media Contact: Paula Cabrera-Crocker, PCCPR Marketing.
Ph/fax: 61 2 9331 3948 Email: PCCPR@bigpond.com
Management: Richard Briggs, Chic Management.
Ph: 61 2 9326 9845 Email: richard@chicmanagement.com.au

MATT ELLIS BIOGRAPHY

Once the front man and founder of hard rockers Sedgwick Pie who supported Reef from UK, Grinspoon and Tumbleweed, Matt Ellis has now been a thriving solo artist for five years. He launched his most anticipated self-titled second album, late 2004.

Since releasing the debut album "Peel" in late 2000, Matt Ellis has rarely come up for air. While the reviewers raved, the audiences packed in and unashamedly screamed for more at his every show. "An intriguing debut from a striking talent" wrote Michael Smith, Editor of The Drum Media. Revolver's Simon Tracy bluntly stated "The songs? Structured but raw and diverse. The playing? Fucking fantastic." Other reviews from Juice, Rolling Stone and The Ozmusic Project affirmed that Peel was "an independent release of the highest quality by a brilliant, emerging Australian artist".

Having prospered around the local live circuit, Matt embarked on tour to reach audiences in the United States and Asia. He performed at venues such as CBGB's Gallery and The Living Room in NYC, and The Gig and The Knitting Factory in LA where he was received with the enthusiasm of his adoring home crowds.

Matt's dedication and ardor reaped in the goods as tracks from "Peel" were played on radio nationally in Australia and College radio in the USA. His songs consistently ranked well on the interactive music charts of sites such as mp3.com, mp3.com.au and ninemsn where "Peel" sat in the top 10 for six weeks, while his own website was trafficked by an average of 10,000 hits per week! The self-produced music video for the title track "Peel" went to air on Foxtel's Music Country, MTV, Rage and Ground Zero and although added to rotation in South East Asia, was soon banned after outraged viewers called in to complain that the clip incited reckless driving. The banning prompted an invitation from Channel [V] Asia for Matt to be interviewed and perform live at the station. Some months later, the second clip "The Cause" obtained similar exposure both locally and overseas.

By October 2002, prolific Matt had written another album's worth of material and was ready to record again. With a production team consisting of long time collaborator (and a musical phenomenon in his own right) Tamlin, ARIA award winner Jonathan Burnside and himself, Matt and his inspired band laid down beds for 12 new songs at Razor's Edge Recording. As a taste of the forthcoming album, a double A-side single of "In This Life/ Where It Starts" was launched in August 2003 to a crowded house in Sydney's Gaelic Club. The Single Guy at The Brag described it as "A lovingly rendered piece of pop melancholia" and The Ozmusic Project said "There are plenty of pop artists out there for whom the form is more important than the substance, but Matt Ellis is not one of them."

2005 is already shaping up to be another frantic year for this restless talent. His website, mattellis.org version 2, has already been launched and is hosting "On Your Way", the first music video from the new album scheduled to be launched in March. The release of the video will be supported by more touring in Australia and overseas. With a spot on the Cockatoo Island Festival on Sydney Harbour at Easter, a showcase at Canada's NXNE Festival in June, the Edge Of The World Festival in Vancouver in July and plans to spend extended periods of time playing in both North America and Europe this year, 2005 could well be the year the world discovers Matt Ellis.

Visit **www.mattellis.org** to uncover more about this unique talent.

Marketing Plan Builder

Use the Marketing Plan Builder template to develop your music marketing plan. At the conclusion of each chapter the Builder will add a new section to assist in the planning process.

Stage nine: Creating press kits

1   Catalogue all external publics with whom your business will come in contact. Prioritise their importance to your business and begin to build and maintain relationships with them.

2   If you are creating a band/artist bio, interview the members using the list of questions provided earlier in this chapter.

3   List all newsworthy events, items and achievements of the band.

4   Make a target list of journalists and media outlets that might be interested in your story.

5   Use an industry directory to compile a list of music industry decision makers who would appreciate receiving your demo CD and press kit. Be careful not to send it to record labels and music publishers who do not accept unsolicited material, as you will be wasting your time and money.

6   Create a press release using the guidelines in the chapter.

7   Try to ensure that the publicity you seek is aligned with the publications you are advertising with.

thebiz – music business portal

www.thebiz.com.au
Download digital version of the
Marketing Plan Builder

Study questions

1   What are **publics** and why are they important to you?
2   What techniques can be used to generate publicity?
3   Is advertising spend related to the amount of editorial space you might receive from a particular publication?
4   Evaluate the bios and press releases contained within the chapter. How well do they adhere to the principles laid out in this chapter? What, if any, improvements would you suggest?

Chapter Ten

WRITING A MUSIC MARKETING PLAN

Learning outcomes

By the end of this chapter you should be able to:
- create a table of contents for a marketing plan
- develop a basic marketing plan
- appreciate strategic marketing planning concepts
- develop elements of a strategic marketing plan.

Introduction to marketing planning

Marketing plans come in many shapes and sizes and strictly speaking, there is no one way of laying one out. Don't be alarmed if the table of contents for a marketing plan you discovered on the internet looks slightly different than the one presented here, since all marketing plans must include certain key elements despite how they are labelled.

This chapter presents a marketing plan format that the authors have used for many successfully implemented marketing projects in both the entertainment and wider business environments.

Before writing your plan

Brainstorming your idea

As discussed in Chapter One, brainstorming is the process of cataloguing all your marketing ideas, product concepts and market opportunities you believe exist for your proposed business. Remember not to pre-judge your ideas – write everything down, even if it seems crazy. Successful marketing plans are often built on grand, sometimes unconventional, ideas, so make sure you capture them.

Scanning the marketing environment – exploratory research

As discussed in Chapter Two, market research can take many forms, and at this early stage in the planning process your focus should be on exploratory research. Meaning, you need to gather secondary information, which is data that has already collected, analysed and published. Usually though, such information was gathered for a purpose not exactly like yours, and thus needs to be filtered in order to meet your specific planning needs.

Elements of a marketing plan

Stratozpheric Chill-out compilation – illustrative example

Bill Smith is the marketing manager of a mid-sized independent record label that is releasing a new compilation album featuring Australian producers, mix engineers and DJs. Bill is required to produce a marketing plan for presentation to the label's board of directors. (*Note:* this marketing plan is fictitious)

> ⊙ ⊙ ⊙   thebiz – music business portal
>
> **www.thebiz.com.au**
> Visit for a digital template of this
> marketing plan.

Executive summary

Approximately 300-500 words in length, the summary assumes that the reader is unfamiliar with the material and thus provides a brief outline of the report's purpose and its major recommendations. If the reader is unfamiliar with the subject matter you can include background information on the organisation that is implementing the marketing plan. This would typically include the company's mission statement, objectives and its broader product/service offerings.

The executive summary goes immediately after the title page, has no page number and does not appear in the table of contents.

Stratozpheric example   **Executive summary**

The purpose of this report is to outline the marketing strategy for the debut release of Stratozpheric, a dance-chill album featuring the work of Australian dance producers, mix engineers and DJs. The objective is to establish Stratozpheric as the leading brand in the Australian dance/chill-out compilation market and achieve sales of 15,000 CDs within one calendar year.

The report will demonstrate a proposed marketing strategy and recommend a course of action that will utilise innovative integrated marketing and promotional tactics, store based as well as electronic distribution, and concise brand management ensuring both the initial success and long-term growth of *Stratozpheric*.

Title page & table of contents

The marketing plan layout presented in this chapter is as follows:

Situation analysis

The situation analysis is the assessment of the current marketplace. It is divided into three major sections: **market situation**, **competitive situation** and **macroenvironmental situation**.

The market situation

The length of the market analysis section depends on the complexity of the market in which you plan to operate. Highly complex markets with many competitors would require detailed study. In this case, you might collect considerable quantities of secondary information, place it in the appendices and then refer to it in brief point form. Broadly speaking, the kind of information required here would include:

- market size in dollars and units over past years
- market growth rates over past years
- major market segments
- trends in consumer preferences, perceptions and purchasing habits.

Competitive situation

Analysing competitors is essential to finding a point of difference between your product and those already in the marketplace. Your unique selling proposition (USP) can only be devised in relation to competitive offerings. If there are many competitors in the market you might wish to group them by size, product/service offerings or location. Otherwise, simply list the companies you will be directly competing with and identify their goals, market position, value propositions, prices, promotional strategies and tactics and distribution methods.

Macroenvironmental situation

This section includes in-depth analysis of four environments within the entire environment. Usually presented in point form, the environmental analysis provides marketing planners with detailed information that will impact on the business. The *Stratozpheric* example presents several issues that will impact not only the first CD release, but also on the viability of future releases under this brand.

Although we have not drawn conclusions from every issue, a real world example would require detailed analysis of each issue. Examples are presented in brief point form covering sociocultural, political/legal, economic and technological issues.

Stratozpheric example   Situation analysis

The market situation

Note: this does not represent a comprehensive market analysis; rather it presents some examples of the type of information that would provide an insightful analysis. Also see Chapter 2 for more information on market analysis.

Trends in the Australian album sales over 2002 included vinyl up 23%, cassettes down 61%, compact discs down 2% and DVD audio up 44%. This resulted in a total decline in unit album sales of 2%. (www.aria.com.au)

Australian repertoire represented 31% of the total ARIA Top 100 album units, up from 15% in the 2003 first half. And 21% of the total ARIA Top 100 single units were by Australian repertoire, up from 18% in the last year's first half. (www.aria.com.au)

Competitive situation

There are several competitors producing major compilation releases. The following recent releases would be regarded as potential direct threats.

Ministry of Noise – Club Mix: A compilation of various local prodcuers and artists. Described as 'the definitive club mix for 2006'.

Cafe Del Car – ChillHouseMix: A mellow mix of grooves and house beats

Sydney – The City of Sun: lazy seaside grooves ideal for summer a daze.

Capriconia One – a local indie label release of local DJs featuring electronic grooves.

Macroenvironmental situation

Sociocultural issues, legal/political, economic issues and technological issues – see Chapter Two.

SWOT analysis

The SWOT analysis is a practical way of cataloguing issues that will impact on your business. A key function of a business plan is to help you assess whether your idea is feasible. The SWOT analysis is a widely used, practical way of critiquing a business idea. It is crucial when completing a SWOT that you be honest with yourself. You cannot afford deceive yourself in your own marketing plan.

Strengths and weaknesses – Issues that affect you personally; issues **internal** to the business or you personally as an entrepreneur.

Opportunities and threats – Issues **external** to the business.

Stratozpheric example		SWOT analysis
SWOT analysis	**Strengths** Unique brand. All-Australian compilation. Appeals to the local desires to hear local artists. National in-store and online distribution.	**Weaknesses** Lack of international tracks. Market may have grown weary of compilations.
Opportunities Utilise online distribution. Emerging local 'sound'. Popularity of new media in young adult target audience. Incorporate live events in the product offering.	**Act now** – capitalise on rising Aussie scene with unique brand that could define the scene. Use new media to capture the imagination of market for online purchase of recordings and live dance events.	Live dance events should counter market resistance to another compilation. Utilise strategic overseas label partners and their international DJ/mix artists to endorse the compilation.
Threats Crowded compilation market. Aggressive competitors. CD piracy. Illegal mp3 downloading.	Unique local release creates strong competitive differences to existing product. Access to both store-based and online distribution may assist in countering downloading. Downloading may in fact assist the promotion of the release, exposing new listeners who might not have heard of the release.	Ensure that the album is full of killer, not filler, tracks. An album of average tracks will not be saved by patriotic Aussies buying the album to support local artists.

Objectives

Organisations need direction. Nothing can be achieved without a sense of purpose. Without objectives business plans become rudderless ships with little chance of successfully reaching a destination. Expanding our discussion of marketing and communication objectives from Chapter Six, let us look at the common features of marketing objectives.

Objectives work best when they adhere to the SMART principle, meaning they must meet the following criteria:

Specific – objectives should not be vague descriptive terms like "our objective is to be the coolest record label in the world".

Measurable – they must be numerically based so they can be measured. Examples include sales volume, sales in dollars, percentage of market share.

Attainable – objectives must be possible within the limits of organisation's resources.

Realistic – similar to attainable. There is no point being optimistic beyond reason. Be aware of your weaknesses by never over-extending your goals.

Timely – objectives must be time based to meet accounting/budgetary cycles.

There are three types of marketing objectives:

1. Sales volume expressed in dollars achieved over time.
2. Market share % gained over time.
3. Return on investment (ROI) expressed as a percentage over a given time period.

Stratozpheric example   **Objectives**

Marketing objectives

- To sell 15,000 units of the compilation in the first calendar year of release.
- 10% of sales (or 1500 units) to be sold via the compilation website.
- 90% of sales (or 13,500 units) via retail distribution.
- These sales figures equate to a gross profit of $245,000, or 15000 units, multiplied by P.P.D. (published price to dealer) See page 131.
- It is extremely difficult to estimate market share for retail music product as there is no quality published data on the issue. The cost of engaging an external market research firm to develop a market share profile would not be cost effective. For this reason market share targets are not possible.
- ROI a figure of 15% is set as the expected return on investment of the total variable cost of licensing, producing and mastering the *Stratozpheric* compilation.

Target audience profiles

Stratozpheric example   Target audience profiles

The primary target market for Stratozpheric is 25–34-year-old urban professional people seeking a sophisticated chill-out compilation experience.

The secondary target market includes the 18–24 year old clubber/dance music fans.

Market positioning strategy

Positioning is how the product benefits are perceived in the minds of consumers. It is what consumers perceive (or believe) to be the benefits of your product compared to those offered by competitors.

Stratozpheric example   Market positioning strategy

Featuring Australia's finest remix and DJ artists, Stratozpheric will take listeners on a journey from the chill-out room, through the languid grooves of nu-jazz, to dance floor territory and back again. Escape your urban mind space – ascend to the Stratozphere.

Creative strategy statement: ***Stratozpheric escape your urban mind space.***

www.thebiz.com.au
Download a Competitor Analysis Worksheet

Product profiles (value proposition)

Aside from the product positioning strategy, which can be loosely described as the **core product benefits**, there are two key components to product profiles:

- **Physical product** a detailed description of the products/services on offer. Includes shapes, sizes, packaging, colours, brands and any other tangible elements of the product.

- **Augmented product** additional services that will encourage customer loyalty. Examples include such things as warranty, service, VIP memberships and invitations to join a street crew.

Stratozpheric example   **Product profiles**

CD compilation featuring 12 tracks by leading Australian dance remix and DJ artists and producers.

DVD featuring music video clips, behind-the-scenes footage of the producers in their studio working environments and career profiles of the artists.

Merchandise – T-shirts, caps, mouse pads, postcards and other assorted merchandise items.

Go-Stratozpheric Live Dance Party
Go-Stratozpheric will be the launch party for 400 celebrities and industry professionals and 100 winners from the Stratozpheric online competition. To be held at a suitably hip inner-city venue, the event will feature the DJs, producers and remix artists from the compilation. Over time it is also envisaged that Stratozpheric will become an annual event on the dance music calendars not only in Sydney, but also in Melbourne, Brisbane, Auckland, Adelaide, Perth, Hobart, Darwibn and Surfers Paradise.

Pricing strategy

A pricing strategy has several purposes.

- To establish the price-to-quality ratio that prospective consumers will use to judge the relative value of your product/service.
- To create a profile of anticipated demand for the product/service.
- To determine the pricing strategies and tactics of competitors and industry price points.
- To establish cost structures of product/service offerings allowing the setting of profitable prices.
- To determine break-even point – the point at which sales are equal to expenses.
- To establish promotional pricing tactics such as discounts and introductory pricing.

Stratozpheric example   **Pricing strategy**

Price – quality ratio
Since the compilation targets Generation X urban professionals, who have a high propensity to spend on leisure, entertainment and lifestyle products, the broad pricing strategy is to maintain a reasonable level of exclusivity, without pushing the product into premium price levels.

A market skimming pricing strategy will be used to ensure that a strong relationship exists in the minds of consumers between the quality of the compilation and its price point. Price discounting and sales promotion pricing tactics will be avoided so as not to diminish brand equity and its critical relationship to price.

Demand profile
Demand for CD compilations seems destined to continue if we look at the success of the recent releases by the major competitors. Capricornia One, for example, a debut compilation with produced sales of 15,000 units. While mainstays of the market Café Del Car, Ministry of Noise and the Sydney – The City of Sun series continue to grow in popularity.

Demand for music appears to be rising despite some distruption in recent years, to major record label sales. Consumers don't seem to care where the music comes from, as long as it is good, reasonably priced and can be easily transferred to portable digital play devices and wireless home entertainment networks.

Competitor pricing and industry price points

The compilation price points of major competitors in the Australian market are:

Ministry of Noise – Clubbers Guide to 2005 (Australia	$31.22
Cafe Del Car – ChillHouseMix	$49.84
Sydney – The City of Sun	$25.95
Capricornia One	$32.99

Stratozpheric CD compilation budget

The following CD production and manufacturing budget represents an approach that might be taken by record labels when calculating costs.

Recommended retail price RRP + GST	33.00
GST (Goods & Services Tax)	3.00
RRP less GST	30.00
Dealers retail margin (40% of RRP less GST)	12.00
Published price to dealer (PPD) including GST	18.00
GST	1.63
PPD less GST	**16.37**
Distribution fee (30% paid to an independent distributor)	4.91
Packaging deduction (25% of PPD)	4.09
Royalty base price (RBP)	7.37
Artist royalty (15% of PPD)	2.54
Mechanical royalty (8.5% of PPD)	1.39
PPD less deductions	3.44
Unit cost of manufacture	2.40
Label gross profit	**1.04**

Note: this is a sample of how a record company could possibly break down the costs of making a CD.

Promotional pricing tactics

In keeping with the premium nature of the products, radical price discounting will be kept to a minimum. However, selected discreet pricing tactics will be utilised to avoid cheapening the established positioning (brand) strategy.

As stated in the product description, the compilation will include a bonus DVD that includes artist profiles and other bonus material. This will enhance perceived value without appearing to be a cheap sales promotional ploy.

Distribution strategy

A distribution strategy outlines proposed methods to move goods and services from points of origin to places where they are purchased and/or consumed. Remember, it is critical that you provide incentives to the organisations and individuals within the channel. What compelling, tangible reasons will you give them to stock, sell, promote or favour your products over competitors?

Stratozpheric example   **Distribution strategy**

In-store distribution
Our existing CD distribution arrangements with GMG Music Distribution will be the cornerstone of the compilation sales performance. As listed in the CD budget earlier, GMG charges a 30% fee calculated on the PPD, or $4.91 per unit.

Performance incentives to music retailers include:
Store managers of major CD retailers will receive free tickets to Go-Stratozpheric live events. In-store, point-of-purchase material will feature heavily in major CD retailers.

An in-store signing event will be staged at a major CD retailer in Melbourne, Sydney and Brisbane and will feature leading artists from the compilation.

On-line distribution
Stratozpheric will be made available on-line via the following means:
• the label's e-commerce website.
• the Australian iTunes website, through an exclusive licensing deal arranged with Apple. The Apple deal also provides for sponsorship opportunities that will be discussed in subsequent sections of this report.

The compilation will not be sold as singles through either our site or iTunes, as the licensing agreements the label has made with the individual artists, their labels and publishers provides for compilation sales only, not singles.

Integrated marketing communication strategy

As discussed earlier, integrated communications is a term that better defines the challenges of promoting value propositions in the contemporary media environment. Merely calling this section advertising or promotion does not take into account the dramatic changes in consumer media consumption preferences.

Integration between the various elements of the promotional mix is critical to ensure consistent and memorable messages that impact on consumers and motivate them to purchase. For precise definitions of each element of the promotional plan, see Chapters Six and Seven.

Stratozpheric example   **IMC strategy**

COMMUNICATION OBJECTIVES

• Build awareness of the Stratozpheric brand within key target audiences and thereby drive sales to meet the stated marketing objective of 15,000 units in year one of release.
• To generate critical support from influential journalists, critics and editors from selected electronica music publications and other pop-culture magazines appealing to target markets.

- To receive high rotation of selected tracks by Triple J, FBI, 2Day FM and other radio broadcasters sympathetic to dance/electronica music.
- To build awareness of the Go-Stratozpheric dance party events, which are an essential element of the entire promotional campaign.
- To increase traffic to website by 20% over existing visitor levels and an average of 1000 hits to the website per week during the release year.
- To expand existing database of email contacts via competitions and online sales by 50%.
- To achieve CD sales to a minimum of 20% of the contacts on the existing database.
- To achieve satisfactory audience ratings from online advertising measures to be supplied by the media vehicle in question.

COMMUNICATIONS STRATEGY

Promotional strategy and timing
While promotional campaigning will be on-going throughout the year of the release, the campaign begins eight weeks prior to the Go-Stratozpheric compilation launch party. It will continue in earnest until four weeks after the release.

The Go-Stratozpheric launch will be held in the first week of November, thus the campaign will begin the first week of September. An appropriate timeline of events will be established to schedule all promotional activities over the 12 weeks of the campaign.

Creative strategy statement
The creative strategy statement incorporates the campaign theme, appeal and major selling ideas.

> *Stratozpheric – escape your urban mind space – with a compilation of new tracks from Australia's finest remix and DJ artists.*

Integration techniques
Central to campaign integration is the overriding campaign theme: "escape your urban mind space – with a compilation of new tracks from Australia's finest remix and DJ artists". This will be conveyed through all copy and artwork, with quality and consistency maintained via a strict style guide developed by the label marketing and creative directors. The Go-Stratozpheric compilation launch and the accompanying web-based competition are the crucial linking elements between all promotional activities.

Promotional budget
The promotional budget is calculated by multiplying expected sales (15,000 units) by $4.09. Note that this $4.09 is taken from the packaging deduction (see CD budget on previous page). The promotional budget is therefore set at $61,350.

PROMOTIONAL MIX

Press advertising: A variety of advertisements to be placed in both glossy and broadsheet magazines and newspapers relevant to key target audiences. Examples include Ralph, FHM, Drum Media, On The Street and Beat Magazine.

Broadcast advertising: The budget allows only minimal broadcast advertising. In-kind arrangements with event sponsors such as pay TV music channels, who will provide discounted advertising and cross-promotional opportunities.

Online advertising: The compilation and the live events will be advertised via the label and individual artist's websites. Additional advertising will be placed on various youth culture websites and those of event sponsors. Cross-media advertising packages will be sought from earlier mentioned print publications, who often provide advertising space on their websites.

Outdoor Advertising: Poll posters will be placed around the inner city in advance of the Go-Stratozpheric launch party.

PR & publicity: CD reviews press kits will be sent to key music critics in all major print publications for review. In addition music journalists with whom the label has solid working relationships with will be invited to Go-Stratozpheric with the aim of getting live reviews.

Guest compare appearances will be made by some of the artists featuring on the compilation. They will appear on relevant programs on the pay TV channels who will sponsor the Go-Stratozpheric event.

Free promotional CDs, merchandise and complementary Go-Stratozpheric tickets will be presented to selected coffee shops, hair salons and beauty therapists in fashionable inner city suburbs. The goal is to get the staff to create a buzz in their clientele who match the demographic target of the compilation/event.

Press coverage, interviews and on-air live performances will be sought from television networks via current affairs and breakfast chat shows. The angle will be the unique 'Aussie' home grown nature of the CD and its role in supporting local artists.

Sponsorship: Sponsors will be arranged for Go-Stratozpheric. Support from media sponsors will be in the form of free/discounted advertising rates. In the case of product manufacturers, complimentary goods will be sought to use as prizes in competitions.

Sales promotion: In-store point-of-sales displays combined with in-store airplay, end-of-aisle displays and listening posts at specialty dance/electronica music stores in/around city locations. Additional in-store promotion from major CD retailers will be sought, which is dependent on current competition for prized in-store placement.

Competitions & data mining: integrating much of the campaign is the competition which will provide VIP entry to 100 winners from the Stratozpheric online competition. All promotional elements will include an invitation to the website to win. Entrants will be asked a series of questions that will 'mine' basic demographic information to be used for future direct marketing.

Sales strategies: Existing label sales executives will implement the in-store promotions as well as in-person approaches to relevant radio DJs and play-list managers for radio airplay support. Additionally, advertisements will be placed in music trade journals that will integrate with sales force approaches and publicity materials targeting non-chain suburban music retailers. Usual support from our existing record distributor will enhance in-store sales efforts.

Direct marketing: Consolidate the email databases of individual artists appearing on the compilation. Combined with the existing label database, this will mean direct contacts of over 5000 names who already receive permission-based email advertising from the label/artists.

SMS promotion: data mining process will also deliver mobile phone numbers to be used in future promotions.

Web / online strategy: The project will feature heavily on the label website, as will the event competition.

Viral marketing: Interns and street crew members will be employed to frequent listening posts at CD retailers and anonymously encourage store customers to 'sample' the compilation.

Packaging: The aesthetics (visual appearance) of all compact disc packaging and point-of-sale material will adhere to a concise style guide in accordance with the creative strategy.

Live promotion: The individual artists on the compilation will promote the music and the Go-Stratozpheric event at their own live performances.

Merchandise: While often an important revenue source, merchandise give-aways will play an important role in rewarding stakeholders, customers and sponsors for their support of the project.

MPLEMENTATION

Project management
The label uses project management software (incorporating Gantt charts) to develop project timelines that ensure all critical processes, events and tasks are met, ensuring the overall success of the project. For a deeper explanation of this process, visit www.thebiz.com.au and download project management templates and Gantt charts.

Control mechanisms
Control and implementation of the integrated communications strategy will be the responsibility of the label marketing manager, who will report to the managing director.

Measuring the promotional plan
The objectives of the campaign are mostly stated as numerically based goals. Sales, web-hits and competition entries are simple to measure. The campaign will achieve them or it will not.

The broader communication objectives of brand awareness will indirectly be measured against sale figures and attendance of the Go-Stratozpheric event. A qualitative brand awareness survey is beyond the resources of the label, and there is no budget to engage an external market research firm to complete this task.

The label will engage an external media monitoring firm to catalogue the editorial coverage in both print and broadcast media vehicles. Radio airplay will be measured by observing chart position on both ARIA and independent dance/electronica charts. Additionally, radio airplay levels can be measured in a more quantifiable manner by assessing performances catalogued by APRA (Australasian Performing Rights Association) whose role it is to collect radio play lists in order to pay royalties to songwriters.

People, partners and process

As mentioned in Chapter One, the authors argue that the most appropriate marketing mix for music, entertainment and arts marketing should include **people, partners** and **process**. Note that more comprehensive coverage on services marketing in the music, entertainment and arts industries can be accessed at **www.thebiz.com.au.**

People

Service businesses rely more than most on the ability of staff to provide an positive service encounter for customers. Remember that a key defining element of services is the inseparability of production and consumption - meaning that front-line staff actually "create" the "product" while at customer simultaneously consumes it. All of us can probably recall both good and bad experiences we have had in service encounters. Whether its a restaurant, dentist, hairdresser or music event, service personnel often are at the centre of either the horror story, or the happy ending.

Partners

Partners are those individuals and organisations with whom your business forms mutually beneficial relationships with. They are not necessarily partners by the strictest legal definition of partnership, rather they are the **networks** that businesses must form in order to survive in ever-increasing competitive markets.

There are many categories used to describe such networks relationships. They include **stakeholders, strategic partners, joint venture partners, alliance partners** and **sponsors.** For more detail on the role of stakeholders in music events see Chapter One - **Music Event & Festival Management.**

Process

Processes are the foundation stones of positive **service encounters**. They are the systems that enable staff to deliver the expected service that customers seek. Importantly, one of the distinctive characteristics of many services is the way in which the customer is involved in their creation and delivery, yet all too often lose who design service process seem to ignore the customer perspective.[1]

Whether your firm is production oriented, or is service-based it is critical that your marketing plan include a **service blueprint.** This simply describes all the key activities required to service the needs of customers in addition to all service encounters they will have with staff from your organisation. Importantly the service blueprint should seek to define process in terms of those that are either (to borrow theatrical terms) **front-stage** or **back stage.** Imagine briefly the highly refined processes that McDonalds has developed to ensure the rapid and consistent delivery of its hamburgers to its customers - theirs is a classic template for developing efficient service processes.

Whether your marketing plan is for a record release such as the Stratozpheric example, or it is for a service-experience based offering, take care to include detailed planning regards people, partners and processes.

Study questions

1   It is said that businesses don't plan to fail, they fail to plan. What is the significance of this statement?

2   What is the purpose of the executive summary?

3   Why is it important for new businesses to complete a fully featured marketing plan?

4   Why is it important for existing businesses to complete fully featured marketing plans?

5   What does the acronym SMART refer to?

6   Why is it critical for objectives to adhere to the SMART principle?

7   Why must care be taken to measure promotional activities?

8   How can the SWOT analysis assist you in developing strategic options for your business?

9.   What is the significance of people, partners and process in designing services

Marketing Plan Builder

Use the Marketing Plan Builder template to develop your music marketing plan. At the conclusion of each chapter the Builder will add a new section to assist in the planning process.

Final stage: Pulling it all together

If all went to plan you will have filled in all Marketing Plan Builders from the previous chapters. Now is the time to collate them and list additional comments, recommendations or ideas that may have emerged during the planning process.

_____

_____

_____

www.thebiz.com.au
Download digital version of the
Marketing Plan Builder

marketing plan builder

Endnotes

Chapter One - References

1 Webster, F.E., 'The role of Marketing and the Firm', in Weitz, B. & Wensley, R. (eds), Handbook of Marketing, Sage Publications, London, 2003, pp.66–82.
2 McCarthy, E.J. Basic Marketing: A Managerial Approach, Richard D. Irwin, Homewwood, IL, 1960.
3 Booms, B.H. & Bitner, Mary Jo, 'Marketing Strategies and Organizational Structures for Service Firms', in Donnelly, J.H. & George, W.R. (eds), Marketing of Services, American Marketing Association, Chicago, 1981.

Chapter Three - References

1 Smith, W.R. 'Product Differentiation and Market Segmentation as Alternative Marketing Strategies', Journal of Marketing, July 1956, pp.3–8.

Chapter Four - References

1 Levitt, T., 'The Best of HBR – Marketing Myopia' (1960), Harvard Business Review, July–August 2004.
2 de Chernatony, L. & Segal-Horn, S., 'Building on Services: Characteristics to Develop Successful Service Brands', Journal of Marketing Management, no. 17, 2001, pp.645–669.
3 Midgley, D.F., 'Towards a Theory of the Product Life Cycle: Explaining Diversity', Journal of Marketing, vol. 45, 1981, pp.109–115.
4 Day, G.S. & Wensley, R. 'Market Strategies and Theories of the Firm', in Weitz, B. & Wensley, R. (eds), Handbook of Marketing, Sage Publications, London, 2003.
5 'The Australian Ballet – Body and Soul Profile', Australian Creative, April/May 2004, p. 9.
6 Starbucks, <www.starbucks.com>.
7 Petrol Records – The Greatest Music Catalogue Ever.
8 Qantas advertisement, The (Sydney) Magazine (Sydney Morning Herald), no. 14, June 2004.
9 Audi advertisement, The (Sydney) Magazine (Sydney Morning Herald), no. 14, June 2004.
10 'About Jet', <www.jettheband.com/band>.
11 Wild, D., 'Official Band Biography', 2004, <http://vr.belowempty.com/bio_official.php>.
12 American Marketing Association, 'Dictionary of Marketing Terms', <www.marketingpower.com/mg-dictionary-view329.php>.
13 Lovemarks, <http://www.lovemarks.com>.
14 Muniz Jr., A.M. & O'Guinn, T.C., 'Brand Community', Journal of Consumer Research, vol. 27, no. 4, 2001.
16 Reuters, 'MySpace Gains Top Ranking of US Web Sites – Hitwise', 11 July 2006, available at <http://today.reuters.com/news/>
17 Thompson, A., 'MySpace Exploration is Marketer's Dream', The Hollywood Reporter, 9 June 2006, <www.hollywoodreporter.com>.

Chapter Eight - References

1 Oxford English Dictionary Online, 2006, <http://dictionary.oed.com>
2 Argyle, M. & Monica, H., 'The Rules of Friendship', Journal of Social and Personal Relationships, vol. 1, 1985, pp. 211–12.

Chapter Ten - References

1 Lovelock, C. & Wirtz, J. "Services Marketing - People, Technology, Strategy", 5th edition. Pearson Educational, 2004.

Index

ABOUT THE AUTHORS

Mark Beard

Mark has taught music business, management and marketing at a number of educational institutes including The Australian Institute of Music, APM Training Institute and JMC Academy in Sydney.

Mark is currently the Marketing Manager of McCrindle Research, a leading Sydney marketing and research consultancy. He also runs his own business, Inblue Marketing Communications, an arts and entertainment marketing consultancy. Mark is also a musician and performer with over 15 years' experience.

Mark holds a Bachelor of Business (Marketing & Tourism) from Charles Sturt University, a Master of Marketing from The University of New South Wales and a Professional Guitar Player Certificate from the Musicians Institute, USA.

Ben O'Hara

Ben O'Hara has taught music industry business at a number of institutions across Australia including the Sydney Institute of TAFE Ultimo, EORA College, and JMC Academy in Sydney and Melbourne. He is currently the course coordinator for Music Industry (Business) at Box Hill Institute in Melbourne.

Ben has a broad range of experience in the music industry, having worked in music publishing and licensing as well as event and artist management. He has also been a performer for over 15 years, and runs his own booking agency, Flower Pot Entertainment Productions, specialising in children's and family entertainment.

Ben holds a Bachelor Arts in contemporary music (Honors) from Southern Cross University and a Graduate Diploma in Management (Arts) from The University of South Australia.

Ben and Mark co-own the online music business resource centre **www.thebiz.com.au**

thebiz – music business portal

Visit the thebiz.com.au for:

- Updates on the topics covered in this book
- Downloadable forms and templates
- The latest music industry news and happenings
- Teacher resources
- More books in the Music Business Series
- Updates from Shane Simpson
- Newsletters and memberships